New Irish Writing

ORIGINAL SINS

Edited by Suzanne Power
and John MacKenna

Published by MACE 2011

ISBN 978-0-9568411-0-0

MACE

CONTENTS

For Maeve O'Byrne

ACKNOWLEDGEMENTS

Project devised and managed by
Suzanne Power

Edited by
Suzanne Power and John MacKenna

Co editing and copy editing
Valerie Ryan and Ilona Blunden

Design, typesetting and front cover original artwork
Julie Lombard

Title
Original Sins (title) created by Mark Turner

Printers
ColourBooks

Printer liaison
Mary Healy and Pat Griffin

Publishers
MACE (Maynooth Adult and Community Education)

ISBN
Shauna Busto Gilligan, NUI Maynooth

Publicity
Rachel Nolan, Jeanne Beary, Eileen Condon, Valerie Ryan,
Martha Woodcock

Posters
Robert O'Brien

Launch
Jeanne Beary, Eileen Condon, Orla Hennessy, Stella Lanigan,
PJ McAuliffe, Rachel Nolan

Distribution
Tim Clifford, Mark Turner, Maura Barrett (Library Service)

Finance
Jane de Montmorency and Steven Thomas

Foreword

The American poet and short story writer Raymond Carver gave concise and sound advice about the process of writing.

'Get in, get out, don't linger. Go on,' he said.

That's what we've been doing over the past four years – working together, as comrades of the pen. Telling stories in the best way we can, then moving on to the next story and the next.

We've been working on novels, short stories, books of non fiction and theatre scripts. We've argued and laughed and read and reread and looked at the work we've been producing from, to quote Joni Mitchell, 'up and down and in and out'.

And always the ambition has been to produce the best writing possible.

We go on writing because sometimes that's all we know how to do, that's what we need and have to do.

And we go on writing with the ambition of being read.

This anthology is a huge step toward the realisation of that ambition.

John MacKenna
2011

Introduction

The writers who feature in this anthology are dreamers who turned their dreams into reality. Kahlil Gibran writes of the tragedy of leaving a page empty: 'Pure was I created and pure will I remain forever...And the sheet of snow white paper did remain pure and chaste forever – pure and chaste – and empty.'

The dream of writing is often so precious, so dearly held, that it is avoided out of a fear of failure. All writers fail. No writer avoids disillusion. But after the essential period of consternation, sometimes despair, the piece pearls and the truth of it begins to shine through the various drafts. The initial inspiration is what fires us all to put pen to paper. The perspiration required to finish a piece is what causes a lot of the initial willingness to abandon the dream. A lived dream is a muddied thing, it is tired, old and dirty by times. But in becoming more familiar to us it allows us to know ourselves all the better and to have the easier breathing of one who has attempted rather than one who has not tried.

The writers John MacKenna and I work with at NUI Kilkenny Campus are our colleagues rather than our students. We have worked with them for four years now and the individuals featuring in this collection have stayed the course literally since the very beginning. Our job is to persuade them of what is already in themselves, to foster it to the point where they no longer need convincing and to leave them alone with their empty pages and time. The writers featured here have learned this and are comfortable with the knowledge. They have a full awareness that pages, when a writer is living their dream, fill with wordplays known only to them and stories only they can tell.

At NUI Kilkenny they share words and stories with companions and receive the kind of criticism that encourages them to write again, in a better way, with more diligence, with stronger inclinations and with a closer affinity to the voice in their head, rather than the voice they think they should hear.

John and I, when we devised the Creative Writing for Publication course with NUI Kilkenny, wanted it to be practical and without pretension, for the benefit of the individual voice in the group setting, for the benefit of the phrase or premise that might be rejected as being 'too easy', 'too simple', 'not what people want to read'. These, we have come to recognise through our own work, are the very things the reader wants. The reader wants to understand their own life and perception through the magnified truth of fiction and memoir. The closer a writer remains to their own truth, their own uniqueness, the better the writer reader relationship.

The writing in *Original Sins* is original and sinful for what it omits as much as for what is written. The writers in this anthology have sharpened their blades for four years and truly learned that less is more on paper, that readers need room to work with the writer in order to own a story with them. They know the value of silence in a story. They use the shadows words cast to great effect. They know they are not students of anything, but writers whose work you will read again. Remember their names. Buy their books.

As their tutors we have learned more than we could ever have taught and gained more than we have ever given.

Suzanne Power
2011

Maura Barrett

I was born in the depths of winter, somewhere in the 1960s. It was an uneventful day on the world stage. My sister describes me thus: 'A flame haired Scorpion with a fiery disposition and a true sting in the tail, which for the most part is kept hidden under a hard body shell and a sweet smile.' I like to read in the sunshine of France, to seek megaliths in Ireland, to sing loudly when no one is listening and I have a thing about monks.

I am privileged to work every day in a Tinsley designed church, with "Meyer & Co." stained glass windows depicting the Beatitudes: *'Blessed are the pure in heart...'*. Not for want, I get wistful. My friends are good. My family is exceptional. I was reared in the Comeraghs and I wrote a book once about Kilcooley Abbey. Oh and I detest potholes.

1

Some Other Beginning's End

by Maura Barrett

This guest room is spacious. Oak frames encase leaded window panes and the pointed ogee arch is outlined in limestone. Tapestry curtains held back with twisted cord remain open. The waxing moon lies on her side beyond, casting eerie shadows over the landscape. The double bed has a pine headboard. An icon of Mary Magdalene graces the wall opposite, and a St Brigid's cross hangs by the bathroom door. I'm grateful the religious imagery venerates women, not being able this night for the might of men.

I hate suitcases. They remind me of Paddington Bear abandoned at the station, lost and forlorn, dependant on the generosity of strangers. Rucksacks are most practical for travelling. I don't have my way much. My husband micromanages, it is an image thing with him. There are suitcases to be seen with after all. A holy water font is placed beside the switch. I like this room, like the simplicity of it.

I sit on the bed with my knees scrunched up. It is cosy and warm. My eyes drift through the window and I stare at the moon. She has a friendly face. Light peeps in gentle tendrils at the edges of the horizon. Just what I need, the churn of nature. When was the last time I just stopped? A hum of monks in prayer serenades me. I watch the night. When the sun rises the moon will say goodbye.

The last few months flash across my consciousness. Keeping busy is a great antidote to life. Thinking is dangerous. It forces your hand. There is a tea light on each window sill. The dawn chorus joins with the men in prayer, gently, melodiously and again I marvel at the wonder of

Mother Nature. The sun on her sky journey gleams life's glow over the land. The trees sway in salute and the limestone monastery glistens in cerulean stone. The daffodils nod as the moon twinkles her farewell. The monks finish their prayer and I watch as they file in procession across the cloistered yard, heads bowed.

Another thing I can not do is become a monk. I've been invited to join them for breakfast, perhaps I will. I feel alive in this dawn flush, I have done it, fled the madness, and the next few days are mine.

Breakfast is simple and delicious, porridge with honey, fruit juice and yogurt. There is a sizeable congregation, and while there are a few old monks, the majority are younger men. I'm not the only guest at breakfast. There is a middle aged couple, Horace and Dorace, I decide; an older woman and two younger men, whom I take to be novices. We eat in silence according to the rule of monastic life. The Abbot says grace and asks the Lord to:

'Grant the gifts of peace and reflection to the guests of Kilcooley Abbey. Make their stay with us a happy and restful time and bring peace to their souls. Amen.'

I can't argue with any of that, it reflects my sentiments. After breakfast I'm approached by Brother Bernard.

'Are you settling in?'

'Thank you, Brother, I slept as soon as my head hit the pillow.'

'Do you have any plans for today? We have lovely walks in the woods, there is a tennis court and we have an Icon Chapel which a lot of people like to visit.'

'As would I, and I can't remember the last time I communed with nature but . . .' I begin.

'Go on, you've started saying it, so you may as well spit it out,' he encourages.

'First I need to do some shopping. Do you know anywhere I can buy a rucksack? I have this suitcase with me and it feels contaminated.'

Brother Bernard is tall and broad shouldered with kind gentle eyes. Bless him, he doesn't even blink. His hair is turning grey while his beard is only dappled in grey yet. His pale robes make him look solid. He oozes wisdom and I don't know his journey but I feel an affinity with him. I hope he doesn't think I'm crazy, though maybe I am.

'Well, there is definitely a bag shop in the city. It happens to be beside a charity shop, both are on Dawson Street. You could offload the suitcase; kill two birds with the one stone. Not that I'm for killing birds you understand? Now I'm away with the birds.'

I laugh at his self-deprecating joke and realise that I haven't laughed in so long. There is a gloom of sadness in my eyes. He says:

'Lunch is at one, if you make it back. I'd be happy to show you around and I'm not an altogether bad listener if you'd like to talk.'

'Brother, I really appreciate that, and I may just take you up on that very kind offer, be warned though, it might make no sense at all.'

'And it might make a lot of sense too,' he speaks softly, 'I could meet you here at 3 o'clock, that will give us loads of time, supper isn't until sixish.'

So I go into town. All seems right in the world. The earth still spins in her axis and my feet are on the ground. My mind is in a cocoon. I don't know the name of that warp, some people call it denial. I offload the suitcase and buy a rucksack. I can't describe the feeling; it's a mixture of guilt and exhilaration. Guilt because I've abandoned the much coveted, monochrome, initialled leather suitcase in the Sue Ryder shop. Exhilaration comes because I actually did.

I feel the liberation of seeking my own counsel; enjoy the freedom of making my own choices. I am like the warrior Queen Maeve, exultingly waving the flag from my chariot after battle.

Who knew that the first steps to self-determination could be found in such an action? There is something else too in the feeling though. The kind of feeling you get when you squeeze a spot, or when you squash a fly. The words 'Fuck him' flail around my head. I am like a bold child, a rebellious teenager and wayward wife all rolled into one. It takes less than an hour, so I wander off and have coffee in a lovely French café. Oh the emancipation of having nothing to do. I bless every woman who has gone before me, Isis, Eve, the women at the Crucifixion, Boadicea, Grainne Mhaol, Emily Pankhurst and a trillion others. Women with prams cruise by the window and I see faces, with features that perhaps I know. What if he is here? I hear again his growl and the blinding sting – **whack**. I flee back to the monastery, before the hub of city life vexes my soul. Just in case.

There is most noble woodland around Kilcooley, where ancient broad leaved trees reign. Pathways invite the feet, birds flutter and sing and there are gentle streams which teem with fish. It is a special place and I am able to lose myself in her thickets and groves. The peace and serenity of its lush fold embrace me like a blanket and I can be still. The sun streams through the leafy screen, while alongside of me in an over-beyond place, the saplings join forces and become an army of shadow. I decide to face it, they are only trees. The challenge demands it. Dense forest and dark places are no match for the new me. It is silent and dark and still, and takes a while for my eyes to adjust. Before me is a portal of light, which I walk towards, am I not being led? The air chills. I hear the rasp of my breath. The portico of brightness gets greater the closer I come to the edge. My boot catches in a bramble. Lurching forwards, decaying pine needles provide a soft place to land. Something glints in a leak of light. I pick up a small object, shiny and round. I scrape away the grit and see that it is a button. It seems I'm not the first to wander this pathless wood. I'm scared now, alert in this dense thicket to danger. I make for the sanctuary of my room. My clothes are sticky in sweat.

The Wreck of the Hesperus confronts me in the mirror. She has a gaunt expression with bedraggled wisps of hair and sunken eyes.

'You didn't get very far did you?' she goads.

'Good Christ, I made it to Limerick, didn't I? All on my own and I got rid of one of his precious suitcases.'

'Oh yeah, that recycled rucksack really reflects your personality, do you even have a personality? It's a straight question. I mean do you have opinions of merit?'

'I know what I don't want,' I whisper.

'Oh right yeah, sure you do. One minute you want to ramble in nature, enjoy the haven of tranquillity this place provides, the next you want to take on a dank airless forest, where no woman should really ever wander alone, and you aren't in there five minutes and you are legging it out of the place with your tail between your legs.'

'But I was tripped – by a trip wire, it was a trap, any sane person would have done the same thing.'

'Any sane person, are you making yourself out to be a sane person? It was only a briar.'

'That's the trouble, I don't know what I am any more, I just know that I'm not this, and I can't be something that I am not.'

'You don't half talk in riddles girl.'

'Well, I'm talking, if it is riddles then that is your interpretation – I can't be what I'm not!'

The steam from the shower hides the Wreck in the mirror.

I, the renewed, brushed off and dusted down, eat lunch in the refectory. As with breakfast, lunch is simple fare. There is cheese and wholemeal bread, fruit and herb teas. I envy the simplicity. I love how the daylight casts rays through the leaded windows, illuminating the dust particles that hang in the air, bestowed from heaven, almost. The monks sing when they pray, haunting Gregorian chants that hypnotise the spirit. My dread in the coppice is carried away on the resonance of those hymns. I eat with relish. There are new guests today, Scandinavians I think, but can't be sure.

Brother Bernard greets me warmly. The corners of his eyes crinkle and it is very beguiling. His smile is a real smile. Roger's isn't genuine and warm. His world is laced with herringbone weave, designer shirts, gold cufflinks and sharp suits. There are leather briefcases, patent shoes, pinstripes, jocular conversations and disingenuous smiles. These smiles take many guises and I know them all. I am soothed by the refreshing essence of Brother Bernard's kindliness. He carries himself with an unruffled dignity. I love how he tucks his hands into the folds of his sleeves. His shoes are soft and comfortable and casual and worn. I want to feel the worn leather at his feet. I think of the Wreck in the mirror and how she would view this with disdain.

'Come,' he says, 'let us take a walk.'

'I would rather not go into that wood.'

'Ah, it isn't for everyone, although I love it myself, it is the seclusion.'

'Actually, I thought the same, before I was tripped.'

'Let me take you around the garden then, there are well trodden pathways there. Tell me, do you have a garden?'

'Oh Brother I do, or rather we do, we've been featured in several horticultural magazines and are the envy of Roger's business friends.'

'Bernard, please, and something in your tone of voice leads me to believe that there is nothing of you in that garden at all.'

I am blown away by those few words. He hears the words and how they are spoken. In this gushing moment of gratitude I take this man into my confidence.

'Actually, there is a grinding stone from a quern stone given to me by an old man who worked on my parents' house. It has a thin pencil like line going through it and is shaped like an egg, I've always loved it, but I fought hard to keep it in the garden, rather, I was indulged and every so often I check that it is still there.'

He reads me as a book, reads every nuance and inflection and between every line of what I share with him and every line that I don't. For three hours I pour out my story. About being the appendage to a wealthy man. A man who is a bottomless pit of insecurity bent on a course of achievement that can never be sated. I am one of those achievements, a trophy, and a possession. He is supposed to be my life and I'm supposed to be grateful. I had been grateful, very grateful when he showered me with attention after my parents were killed. Grateful for love, any love.

'And then there is the Wreck in the mirror, the one who told me to leave in the first place, the same one that provokes me now.' I falter.

'Sit with me,' he says. 'Thank you for unburdening yourself. Do you know that suitcase you got rid of this morning?'

'Yes?'

'Can you visualise yourself putting all of that 'stuff' into it, locking the clasp and burying it deep in a hole in this garden?'

'I'd love to burn it on a pyre,' I say.

'So do,' he says.

In my dreams I raise a mammoth bonfire. I place the suitcase atop and fan the flame of its extinction. It blazes a fierce fire, a fire so hot that I have to step away. It hisses and cackles and rages and spits. It leaves cindered chards of charcoal in a circle on the green like a blot on my soul and I wonder if it is a venal or a mortal sin and if I have come close to the fires of hell.

'No, you haven't,' Bernard reassures, 'and there was no sin in that.'

Later still I soak in the bath and feel the sanctuary of the place wash over me. I glow in the tenderness of simple gestures and in the relief of not being found. There is glory in whole days to myself, no one to disapprove, no tuts and no frowns. The Wreck in the mirror is covered with the hand towel. I sleep like a baby.

I ache in the new day. My eye swells, my jaw hurts. The Wreck in the mirror confronts the harridan looking back.

'Go back to him,' she implores.

'Every new beginning comes from some other beginning's end,' I reply.

A Magic Key

This welcome retreat from the din of lunchtime is an anomaly. Once thought on, it forces out the creaks, the coughs, the footfall, the thud of a closing door. How do you write silence? I hear the scratch of my scrawl. Then I don't. By magic I find a key and slip through the invisible membrane into the kingdom of silence.

A Question of Attraction

I know he likes me. I know he struggles with it. I also know his wife. The door opens and somehow I just know that he is there. I look up, it is him.

'Ah Peter,' I say, 'You'll not believe what I'm researching here.'

'Show me,' he says.

He slips round my desk and looks at my PC. The screen displays a book jacket, *A Map of Glass* by Jane Urquhart. A woman fishes beside a clear blue lake.

'I have that here – snap!' he says proffering the book.

I feel myself shudder. He sits against the desk.

'That's too weird,' I say.

'I find it comforting.'

'Comforting?'

'Yes, it makes it synchronistic, like it is the hand of destiny.'

There is silence. I can hear his breath. I dare not make eye contact. I'm scared. Scared that to look would expose the attraction. Why does he have to be so bloody self-assured?

'Have you made any New Year's resolutions?' I ask.

'To be good,' he says, 'but I also plan on remaking it next year.'

'Thanks for the book,' I say.

I feel him looking at me, and I'm glad that the moment has sort of passed. Still in the throes of a panic, I remain seated.

'Let me take you to the lake on Monday,' he says.

'That should be grand, but best check in with me again on Monday morning,' I say.

Jeanne Beary

As the only girl in fifth class not to knit a jumper, I have known failure, learned to persevere (eventually managing a hole ridden scarf!) and to enjoy success when it comes. I have never been reclaimed as a king's long lost daughter (sorry Mum and Dad!), nor learned to fly with a dressing gown around my neck, nor discovered how to read other people's minds but my childhood dream to be a writer is something I have made a reality. In the cocoon of this writing group, I was nurtured, supported and sheltered, until ready to emerge and display my efforts.

I am privileged to work with wonderful children in Bunscoil Bhríde, Rathangan. I live in Naas with my husband, Denis, our two children and our dog, Shirley Basset.

One of my stories was shortlisted for the Francis MacManus Prize 2010 and another recorded for 'Stories for the Ear' 2011.

2

World Without End

by Jeanne Beary

Glory be to the Father, and to the Son. Icy metal presses against the cheek of the left buttock. Hard and cold, it imprints its form, stamping its mark on skin and flesh. Sitting rigidly, features are set to assume a gormless expression. One flicker of guilt makes pretence futile.

'Halve the distance between yourself and Martha,' my teacher commanded earlier. We stood obediently in front of the class, facing each other. 'Now, halve that distance again.'

I stepped forward for a second time. Martha lay within reach. She looked as if she had a bad taste in her mouth; her expression turned increasingly sour the closer I came. Piggy red curls clipped around a freckled moon face. I am sure Martha is neither pretty nor clever; her confidence in being both leaves me doubting myself. Hours must be spent every evening in preparation for Martha's next day at school. There'll be reading with Martha, followed by checking spellings, tables and editing her written work. The next day's lunch will be prepared. Her uniform will be washed. Her tie lacks elastic; around here it's the biggest sign that somebody actually cares. Each evening as I herd my younger sisters by we witness her mother waiting at the gate to hug, kiss and pore over test results.

'Halve the distance again,' I was instructed. Martha turned her face away and leaned slightly backwards. Someone giggled. The teacher coughed and glared, then surrendered. 'Sit down Martha.'

Her tone was as if she was bored of a spoiled child. It meant no smirks for Martha as she returned to her seat. Without pausing the teacher took Martha's place and nodded at me in support. I smiled shyly back.

'If you keep halving the distance between Karen and me,' she gestured me forwards and I took another step, 'she may keep getting closer but she will never actually reach me. We can keep dividing that space by half forever and ever and ever,' her hands moved about, 'and it will never become nothing. It will always be there.'

'But Miss Rooney, it must get really tiny and eventually disappear,' a voice called.

'It will get minuscule but it will never end, it can always be half as small again. Just as numbers can always be bigger they can also always be smaller. This space may become less and less but it will go on infinitely.' On the board she drew an eight toppled over. 'Forever.'

As she pointedly thanked me for my 'mature participation' in her lesson we heard the cry.

'It's gone! Miss Rooney, it's gone!'

I hold my breath as the teacher scans our number. Her eyes rest on one or two of us but resume their journey. She purses her mouth; the prayer commences. Gasping for air, I join in loudly. The droning of the thirty-two of us reminds me of a gang of witches huddled around a cauldron. We are praying for honesty and goodness to win out, for the sinner to repent. And to the Holy Spirit as it was in the beginning, is now and ever shall be, world without end.

His footsteps can be heard reverberating against black and wine diamond patterned tiles long before he enters the room. The two sent to retrieve him arrived back moments ago delighted at having successfully completed their mission, excited by the forthcoming drama. Well soled shoes make an ominous click-clack as he strides along the cavernous corridor. He opens the door with authority. Every room is his room and yet none of them are. The teacher recognises that the star performer has arrived and grants him centre stage, shuffling to the corner. Maintaining a position in the wings, she readies herself to eyeball us if we don't look at him with sufficient adoration or if attention is not paid. Even in shame and dishonour we have to pretend to be very good girls.

Pushing his glasses up his nose and adjusting his white collar he begins:

'A horrible thing has been done today. Somebody has taken something which was not hers to take. There is a thief in our midst. Somebody took – ' he pauses to look at our teacher.

Caught off guard her prompt is slow, 'Alison's necklace.'

'Alison's necklace.' He addresses the injured party. 'Alison, where did you have it last?'

'In my pencil case, Father. And now it's gone.' She holds up the empty tin as proof.

'What does it look like?'

'It's a gold cross, Father. I got it for my Confirmation. My Mam's going to kill me.'

'It's disgraceful that here in a class where you have all newly received the Sacrament of the Holy Spirit, you would tarnish that occasion by violating the Lord's Commandment: Thou shalt not steal.' Pronouncing it with relish, he draws out the words for effect, looking at each of us as if he could melt us with just a thought.

'I am going to ask each girl in this class a question and I want each of you to answer truthfully. Do not compound the sin by lying. Liars do the work of the devil.'

He addresses the first girl. 'I warn you not to bear false witness. Do you know who took the necklace?'

A slightly shaky 'No.'

The same answer is repeated until we reach Sharon. Sharon is definitely not a suspect. She looks dubious. 'I don't think so.'

Our teacher rolls her eyes.

'What do you mean 'you don't think so'?' The priest demands. 'Did you or did you not take it?' Each word punched out with a world of space between.

Sharon gets flustered. 'Yes, I mean, no, I mean I didn't take it. I mean, I don't know who did.' With her hand raised like a student, the teacher waits for her turn to speak. Father Harrigan ignores her.

'Well then why didn't you answer 'No' like everyone else? I'll ask you again, did you or did you not take Alison's necklace from her pencil case?'

Sharon stays silent but shakes her head.

'Did anyone see Sharon near Alison's pencil case?' It's addressed to the class.

Our teacher answers instead, using a technique of school and stage, information relayed in a loud voice, scratched to resemble a whisper. It carries clearly to all our ears.

'Em, excuse me, Father. Sharon was in resource.'

'When it happened?'

The teacher nods, mouthing: 'All morning.'

We are stuck; nobody has admitted guilt so everyone is a suspect. I'm desperate for a pee but I can't risk reminding them that I am here; I cross my legs and hope he leaves soon.

'I would like the girl who took the necklace to own up now.' Silence reigns. 'There is a thief in our midst. Everybody take out your bags and empty them. Put everything on the desk. Open your pencil cases and your lunch boxes.'

The rustling and rattling as thirty-one girls unpack belongings for inspection drowns out the conversation. Father Harrigan moves to consult first with the teacher and secondly with the girl who is now without her necklace. Alison begins to cry and we quieten to hear.

'Why on earth did you take it off? What was it doing in your pencil case?'

It happens all the time, when the villain is too intimidating or can't be identified, the victim gets blamed. The silent message is that you somehow deserve what you get. Maybe.

Plastic lids are peeled from containers. As the sandwich smells of egg, onion and fish pollute the room, I take out my own lunch. My bread and jam is innocent. Sort of.

In my home we call it finding. We are encouraged to find things, little things, big things, all manner of things. It has been this way forever.

'Look what Karen found today,' she'd praise, showing my loot to my father. He was the marker for how well you'd done. Normally he'd cast an eye over your haul, grunt and move to the fridge for another beer but if you found something good, he'd pick it up, weigh it in his hand and tell you what a good girl you were. Then he'd put it in his pocket and take it with him to the fridge and wherever he went after that. The remainder would be split up, food stored in the kitchen and knick-knacks put in the drawer, which my stepmother keeps for our treasures. Once they're handed up, she looks after them.

'In case the baby would swallow them and choke.'

The baby resides in the activity station Dad found in someone else's front garden as we were driving past a couple of weeks ago. I often find stuff for her without taking anything – toys on pavements, soothers in the aisles of shops, dropped and abandoned items that clean up like new after a good wash.

I don't always hand everything up. Sometimes I keep things to myself, like money, it's best not to hand up money. It seems to make everything worse. My sisters and I are good at finding things; despite the jumble strewn around our house, without our scavenging the food presses would be completely bare.

Yesterday, after I sent my sisters walking home together, I found two pots of jam, a small loaf of bread, two bananas and a pack of yogurts. The yogurts were given to me because I helped a lady pack her shopping into her car. I also found some nappies in the toilets at the entrance to the doctor's surgery. The rest I acquired by visiting three shops on the way home while carrying my schoolbag. I walk with my eyes on the street, unearthing bronze and golden cents, two toned euro, sometimes even notes. If the supermarket is quiet, I get down on my hands and knees and reach in under the shelves, collecting a fortune. Then I pay for the crackers as I leave with cheese, a jar of baby food, three potatoes, ketchup and crisps – two bags out of a six pack means it's a while before anyone notices – all hidden out of sight.

The worst thing I ever took was a pair of earrings; I took them from someone I liked. That someone is trying out for best understudy as she bids Father Harrigan farewell; the 'slán' is in her best Irish accent. Despite the many bananas, apples and mandarins now being repacked into lunch boxes, it has been a fruitless search.

'Hopefully someone will choose to do the right thing,' Miss Rooney says loudly for our benefit more than his, 'please God, it will turn up before the end of the day.'

The earrings were square studs, the gems too large to be expensive, but the silver was stamped, so I knew it was real. She had taken them off for PE and left them on her desk. They were gone on her return. Six girls had left the hall to use the bathroom. All of us had sworn we hadn't touched them. She searched our bags and belongings to no avail.

'Anyone could have come in,' we had insisted, 'it must have been girls from another class.'

Eager to believe us, she let the matter drop. My Dad smiled when he saw them, showing brown, pitted teeth.

'Girls,' Miss Rooney lowered her stool, moved it into our midst and sat down. 'There's something I need to say. You know the way you visit your friends' houses and they do things differently to the way you do them in your own?'

We nod; those who get invited to other houses know what she is talking about. 'We have different types of meals; some mums work, some dads work. In some houses bedtime is eight, in other houses nine.'

'I don't go until ten,' Sharon shouts.

'Thank you, Sharon,' she continues, 'all homes are unique, but in some households very different rules apply. Good children live in these houses. Good children who were born the same as you or me but were unlucky that they live in homes where they are taught to do things that aren't nice.

I remember once when I was at school there was a girl whose family taught her to steal. I know you'll find it hard to believe because your Mum and Dad would be really upset if you were caught stealing…'

'Mine would kill me,' someone agrees.

'…but this poor girl was expected to take things. Instead of getting into trouble for taking things, she was in trouble if she didn't. She knew that what she was doing was wrong but in her house it was right. Nobody gave her a chance. Maybe there are girls in our class who have families like that. I don't know. I don't know what happens in your homes.'

We laugh but she remains focused. 'The girl who took Alison's necklace needs to leave it back because she knows she should, not because we can make her. She can leave it anywhere she likes; we won't mind once we can find it. If it's returned, she'll have won. Despite what she's learned at home, she will have done the right thing.' She sounds sincere yet I doubt her.

I excuse myself to go to the bathroom. Foul smells linger. I move to the disfigured looking glass hanging on the stained wall. I look in. Two white circles behind the glass interfere with my reflection. Like rings etched by a hot cup, they lie side by side. My hair is dull and greasy, as is my skin, which is peppered with little spots. I stare into dark brown eyes. My pupils are mirrors, reflecting a smaller version of myself – no spots, lank hair or tatty uniform can be detected. Lying within the eyes of that little me, is an even tinier me. Its minuscule eyes hold a microscopic version of myself that I can't see but I know must be there. I may get less and less but I will go on infinitely, and though I can't actually view myself, it doesn't mean that I don't exist. I wash my hands and shake the water from them. Drops fly. Some land on the reflection of my face, where they snake their way downwards.

The day lingers on with still no sign of a cross and chain. Alison starts crying again as we pack up our belongings. Loud sobs are met with Miss Rooney's silencing stare and become sniffles, muffled by Alison's sleeve. The girl sitting next to her rubs her back while giving me and some other girls a real dirty look. Alison keeps snivelling. A girl bursts into the classroom bearing the cross in her hand, its chain dangling.

'I found it Teacher, on the floor, in the bathrooms! I found it.'

Alison takes possession of her necklace like an Olympic gold medallist; the teacher smiles brightly at all of us. They bask in their moments of glory. We line up to leave the class when I spot the pencil case, lonely, unnoticed on the floor. A tag hangs from the zip bearing the name Martha in a heart. It is pink, fluffy and expensive looking. Amen.

Unwelcome Silence

There's no such thing as silence. The quieter you are, the more you hear. In our writing group there's a swish of hands over paper as pens impart ideas, muddying once clean pages. Fabric chafes as someone uncrosses their legs. A table creaks in protest as it supports an elbow. Alone and still, silence continues to evade us. There's the gentle gulp as you swallow. You hear the air as it travels in and out of your lungs. Your ears buzz with a tinny sound as you concentrate. The soft thud of your heart proves that you are alive, still present. When it stops there will be silence, not because noise ceases but because you will no longer hear it. You will have been silenced. Listen and live until the silence comes.

First Sins

We listen carefully as the door creaks, shuttering Susan, the sinner, in the dark. We hear the scrape of warped wood being forced along a furrow and then whispers. With the exception of our teacher, Jenny and I are closest to the box and we're having a great evening.

'She said nothing,' Jenny murmurs.

'What do you mean she said nothing?'

'Well she got to the "These are my sins bit", and then she went straight into the act of contortion. She didn't tell him any sins.' The teacher looks worried. She must be listening too.

'I don't think it makes any difference,' I hiss, 'I made all of mine up.'

'I know. How can you have fought with your brothers and sisters? You haven't got any.'

'Well I said: 'I didn't do what my Mammy asked me' and 'I didn't do what my Daddy asked me'. Then I was stuck. I needed something else to say.'

With the screech of protesting hinges Susan emerges. The teacher takes her aside and talks quietly to her.

'Do you think she's in a load of trouble?' I ask.

Again there's the sound of wood chafing. Jenny shrugs, busy eavesdropping on the next girl's wrongdoings. The teacher leads Susan by the hand. They shuffle past us and Susan is pushed back into the confession box. Jenny watches in amazement.

'That's so unfair! How come she gets to make her First Confession twice?'

Ilona Blunden

I'm lucky my father changed his mind about becoming a priest. My name is often a handy ice breaker (it's Hungarian for Helen). I'm from Dublin, the youngest of four, and live with my husband in Kilcullen, Co. Kildare, somewhere I thought was halfway to Killarney as a child.

I was a seventeenth-century French queen surrounded by musketeers in a magazine ad for computers. I rode the white horse that played Tír na nÓg in *Into The West*. When I was ten I became Alice in Wonderland on stage; 'Curiouser and curiouser!' has inspired me ever since. Thanks to a working life in communications, I get to write every day.

Winner of the Cecil Day Lewis Poetry Award (2004). Highly commended in the National Writers' Group of the Year Award (2008). 'The Anniversary', a short story, has been selected by the Kildare Arts Service for broadcast in 'Stories for the Ear' (vol. 2) launching in May 2011.

3

Wonderland

by Ilona Blunden

The letterbox snapped. Claire ran to pick up the post. In the middle of the pile she noticed another hand drawn envelope. She stared at the colourful piece of art in her hands. She ran her fingers over the tiny lettering, intricate drawings and images cut out from magazines. As usual it took her a few seconds to find her name and address hidden in the picture.

Part of the envelope was wet from the rain causing the ink to run, leaving an indigo streak through the orange sun in the corner. Claire sniffed the envelope. She detected the faint scent of hash. Tom must have created his latest cover in one of Amsterdam's special coffee houses. She shoved the envelope into her dressing gown pocket. So far her parents hadn't seen any of them; she always got to the post first.

Claire went up to her room and pulled out the old fashioned hat box from under her bed. She laid out all the envelopes she had received so far and placed the new one in the centre. She marvelled at Tom's extraordinary talent and thought he should have his own exhibition.

She loved the anticipation of each envelope's arrival. Once, three came a few weeks apart and when she put them side by side they fitted together like a jigsaw to form a whole new picture. She couldn't quite believe someone would spend hours creating something so unique just for her.

She pushed two of the envelopes together allowing a grand staircase to appear with a portrait of a woman at the top of the stairs. Claire's name and address were on the cover of a book that sat on a table at the foot of the stairs. Another envelope was divided into squares with images filling each one like a visual charm bracelet: musical notes, a candle in a window, a camera, an apple tree, a kiss. Another showed her name and address set out in the squares of a crossword. Her name was always embedded in the pictures as if she were part of the story.

One envelope had been transformed into a rectangle of winter blue sky with tiny dots of Tippex for the flurry of snow and a single black diagonal line. The handwritten words across the top didn't make sense. A week later its companion arrived. More disjointed words and the same winter scene except the black line continued, turning into a telegraph wire with a smiling cartoon crow perched on top. Claire put the two envelopes together and found herself humming along to a tale of hearts and bypasses, smiles and madnesses from *Blackbird on The Wire*.

His letters read like Kerouac on crack. All about his adventures with women. He would start a letter and pick it up again after a night out: it was nine thirty in the morning and he'd been drinking since midnight. He borrowed some clothes from his new flatmate without her permission. He tried to sneak them back while she was out but got caught. She didn't see the funny side.

The first time Claire met Tom he was wearing red plimsolls, his jeans were ripped at the knee and he kept pushing his Cure-head hair out of his eyes. She was seventeen and in her last year at school. He was a carpenter and a big Smiths fan. She would not have been surprised to see a daffodil hanging out of his back pocket. He hung out with artists, writers and photographers. There was always music playing in his house. He had artist's hands, roughened from long hours working with wood. When he spoke his accent was a mix of Irish, Dutch and English, mangled from years spent wandering between Dublin, Amsterdam and London.

Everything about Tom reminded her of Dr Seuss. He was endearing and eccentric. He was doing up his house one chair at a time. Nothing was finished. She couldn't explain it, but she always felt safe there, cocooned in warmth and kindness. There were no rules, no curfews. Tom's house was her Wonderland.

A letter arrived just before Claire's twenty-second birthday. A black painted crow sat in the centre of the envelope. It looked like the same crow she had seen before but this time it was in distress: its eye white with fright, the texture feather like too. Tom had added bits of fabric to heighten the effect. Her name and address were typed in black over the red 'blood' pouring from its wing.

Tom's letter explained how he had decided to move back to Amsterdam. He was leaving in a few days. His work gave him the freedom to live anywhere and he would always be busy as long as the demand for Shamrock Bars was high. He invited her over for what he called their Last Supper.

She watched him drop a riot of peppers into a pan on the cooker in the tiny kitchen. He opened a bottle of red wine that he had been saving and poured it into two mismatching cups. They ate in the living room with plates on their laps in front of the fire. Claire sat, mesmerised by the flames. Tom picked out a CD. The plaintive notes of Jeff Buckley's *Last Goodbye* filled the small room.

'Here's to you Claire, catch-22 and all grown up.'

She laughed at Tom. Maybe it was the wine, or maybe it was turning another year older, but something made her realise that she was losing more than a friend. She did feel all grown up. She would start a new job the following week. She could afford a car. She could move out of her childhood home and rent for the first time. Things would never be the same again. Wonderland would be a thing of the past.

Hundreds of photographs took up half a wall in Tom's living room, documenting his travels and the people he met along the way. Girls laughing and smiling for the camera. Tom caught her sideways glance.

'At least two of them were the real thing. I didn't give up on them, they gave up on me. And so here I am,' Tom said with a grin.

There he was, thought Claire, alone but smiling.

A ray of evening sun lit up a giant fish bowl on the small table in the corner. It was filled to the brim with rolls of undeveloped film.

'Don't you want to know what's in them?' She asked.

'I've been collecting them for years. Why don't you pick one and surprise me?' Tom smiled.

Claire had trouble sleeping that night. She dreamt she was running to catch up with Tom but could never reach him. Everything was made out of plasticine: bus stops, sign posts, post boxes. Even the pedestrian crossing was like a long liquorish allsort with two giant gobstoppers for beacons. Tom would turn and run backwards, smiling at her, but he always disappeared around a corner before she got there, followed by a string of smiling mice and crows. *There is a light that never goes out* was playing on a loop.

Claire wipes a layer of dust off the lid of the old hat box and looks at the envelopes for the first time in almost ten years. She runs her fingers over their uneven surfaces. She inhales, her nose almost touching them. The letters smell of old smoke and ash from years of storage. The kind of smell that never goes.

She takes some out of the box and spreads them like playing cards on her kitchen table. She picks up an envelope. It has an ink drawing of some Chinese despot she can't name. She pulls out the contents. It's dated April 1988. Tom is just back from a party in Chelsea. Must have been a good night. He's met someone new. She still can't pronounce her name. Tom tells her not to worry, there is life after school. Claire smiles.

The giant cartoon chicken in red and white socks catches her eye. It's postmarked 1993 from London. She opens the letter. Tom wishes her luck in a new job and tells her about the coffin he found in an alley to go with the baby's cot in the living room. He's calling it 'From the cradle to the grave'.

She picks up another one. The blind albino mouse is off on his travels again, with his signature Blues Brothers hat and shillelagh. Ghosted underneath are bars of music and a tiny map of Amsterdam beside the stamp. It's dated December 1997. He's met someone new and thinks she could be the one. Claire remembers being happy for Tom. He tells her he's sorry for the loss of her father. It was Tom's last letter. Until today.

She studies the new envelope closely and feels the familiar rush of excitement at its arrival. Not a mouse or crow in sight, but a nod to Warhol with an array of shimmering seahorses and starfish set out in his infamous grid design. She notices the stamp as she opens the envelope and unfolds the letter. It reads: 'I'm home! Here's my new address. Want to catch up?' She smiles.

She reaches further into the box, delving under the envelopes, and lifts out a set of prints. She flicks through the series of black and white images. They tell the story of a girl in her late teens laughing for the camera and almost falling over in flared dungarees and platforms. Claire slips the photographs into a plain envelope with Tom's new address on the cover and writes 'Surprise!' on a Post-it.

She arranges the still bright envelopes inside a large wooden frame. She presses the glass down firmly, trapping musical notes, black crows, albino mice, penguins, pianos and sea creatures. She lifts the frame, carries it into her study and hangs it on the wall opposite the window.

Life Breath

It is late winter and we all recognise the need for silence. It is our life breath. It comes before stillness. After that, our words flow and our stories come alive on the page.

Little Sins

We commit our minor indiscretions every hour. Little sins seep from our pores and are washed clean away. Just a light stain remains on the soul at the closing of each day.

Nora Brennan

I retired early and years later, woke to the blank page. When I joined a creative writing group, it was as though spring arrived. New shoots appeared; words tumbled onto pages. Some I've nurtured and they have grown and blossomed. Others are buried in weeds. Daily I'm tempted to turn my back on the garden. Yet I know the joy that summer brings and a poem published is a flower pressed between the covers of a book. I'm inspired by the everyday and my love of the land stretches back to the days of my childhood growing up on a farm outside Inistioge. My poetry has been published in The Stony Thursday Book, Kilkenny Broadsheet, Revival and Boyne Berries; my creative non fiction in Ireland's Own magazine. I was runner up prize winner in the 2009 Ireland's Own Creative Writing Competition memories section, published in Ireland's Own Anthology 2010.

4

One Breath

by Nora Brennan

It was the season of Zubes. Except there were none and the best I could get was a packet of Fisherman's Friend; those little fiery marbles I thought would banish bugs up my nose and out through my ears. My chest could not be silenced all winter and I heard it muttering to itself even when I lay down to sleep. I had finished two courses of antibiotics and several packets of the fiery Friend. And deliberated. One day I was calming the anxious child who believed it was serious, another day I was coaxing the sleepy woman who remained in denial. These two characters coexisted in the air pockets of my lungs over the previous months. Just as I expected to be put on more antibiotics, the doctor suggested x rays.

It was nine years before when the surgeon told me I had abnormal cells in the breast tissue. He slipped the word malignant into the conversation as if I wouldn't notice. I don't remember much else about the interaction but it was a sunny day and the venetian blinds seemed to contain the sun's vitality while I was in that room. I went to the garden centre afterwards. Home felt empty and the thought of the phone ringing jarred. It was April and plump bodied plants were displayed all around. The central table under the Perspex roof was filled with pots of forget me nots. I had an urge to buy a dozen there and then, give them to family and friends as I told them the news: I was on the way out but if they planted the forget me nots, I'd be back, regular as the cuckoo in May, out of sight but rooted in their gardens. I bought one for myself instead.

Shortly afterwards I had surgery and a flurry of friends and relatives came to visit. They brought get well cards and Mass bouquets and told me it was all down to positive thinking. I didn't think much but kept on working in Hanrahan's drapery. When a large department store from Dublin took over, I was sidelined for assistants half my age. There was something surreal about not going to work and it took me a while to register the fact that it didn't matter when I had coffee or lunch. I hadn't expected loss to plunge so deep or the life I had known to be scooped out of me so swiftly. Contacts dwindled and I saw less of friends. When our paths crossed, I knew their lines before they started.

'I'll give you a buzz' or 'I meant to phone you, I've been sooo busy.'

People told me I should play bridge or work in charity shops. I got Sally instead. She was the only living creature who didn't have a list of suggestions about how to beat cancer. And she had no neat stories about women diagnosed with breast cancer decades before who were still alive.

The years that followed were filled with grace. I found nature in the way some people find God though I don't suppose there's much difference. Sally brought me outdoors every day and I began to see more of the trees and sky. She made lots of friends in the park and had many admirers. We got to know each other's oddities and quirks around the house and if I was out without her, I'd be eager to return, always with a smile on my face.

There was a quietness in the hospital waiting room that I had never experienced in the GP's surgery, as if the air was toxic and the only way to survive in it was to keep your mouth shut and breathe less. I scanned the walls in search of something to read. I studied dressing gowns and slippers, a man fixated on the vinyl floor, a woman flicking pages at a furious pace. When my name was called, I rose fast as the hand of the brightest pupil in class. I was all eager, hoping I'd win favours and get a good report.

'You can change in here' the woman said, drawing back the flimsy strip of fabric. 'Take off everything except your pants and wear this with the opening to the back. I'll call you.'

She handed me a wisp of material and left. There wasn't enough space in the cubicle to sit so I stood facing the poster of a pregnant woman on the wall. She had a bubble floating out of her stomach that said: 'Have you told staff about me?' I was all bones in the tight space and held on to my elbows, wishing I didn't have to leave.

'Now Maria, come through,' the woman said peeping into the cubicle. I followed her into a darkened room full of machines. A small two step ladder helped me onto the couch. The coldness of the room pierced me and my bones felt frozen.

'It's painless, just a few slides and we'll be finished.'

I knew how easy it was to be fooled by so called painless procedures, how radiation could singe a body at a glance. The woman's eyes were focused on machines and she positioned them in a way that if one didn't snap me, the other would.

'Big breath in, hold it,' I heard her say when she disappeared behind a glass wall. 'And out. Breathe normally.' I was anxious about her instructions and wondered if I had taken in enough breath. She hurried back, rearranged me and repeated the instructions. I thought surgery would have been merciful by comparison. I'd have been oblivious to what was going on, doctors and nurses talking about the foreign body before their eyes that looked brazen enough to take over my whole system.

She removed a number of black plates and said:

'I'll be back shortly.'

I was weary counting chrome squares on the ceiling when she returned.

'We need to take a couple more pictures,' she said in the same detached voice. By the time she had finished, I was footless as a mermaid, doing a deep sea dive inside her lens and imagining rare clusters everywhere I turned.

I left the cold room feeling done and dumped as though I was microchipped and could be tracked down anywhere. The cubicle had lost the secure feeling it had earlier and I hurried into my clothes, gathering the remains of myself from the hook on the wall.

One week later, I was sitting in the consultant's room.

'I'm sorry to have to tell you the cancer has spread,' he said. 'The scans have shown up secondaries in the lung and bone.' I sat there as though my insides were washed away and his voice was nothing more than an echo on a distant shore.

'How bad?' I asked in a detached voice.

'It's grade 4. We can treat it with chemotherapy. But there's no guarantee.'

'How long will that give me?' I hadn't expected him to know where the next pirate raid on my body might be.

'Six months at most.'

'And without treatment?'

'About three months. We can't be certain. It will have side effects. Take a few days to think about it and discuss with your family.'

'I don't need any time to think about it. I won't go down the road of chemotherapy again.'

'I fully understand. If you change your mind, we'll get treatment underway. And if you don't, we'll do all we can to help make you comfortable.'

That was all I wanted to hear. Just to know I wouldn't be left scraping the walls in pain.

'I'll write to your doctor and the staff here will notify the home care team.'

'Thank you for all your help,' I said getting up from the chair. The soft innocence of his handshake was the only thing that felt real to me as I left the room.

That night I felt I had a wormery inside me. I made regular trips to the bathroom and each time I got back into bed, I kept holding on to my body just to know it was still there. I slept fitfully and dreamt about the nuns at school and the little prayer they had framed on the corridor.

'*All shall be well, and all shall be well, and all manner of things shall be well.*'

It didn't mean anything to me at school except I used to say the words every time I turned the corner and saw them outside Sr Josephine's office. I repeated them throughout the night and wondered about Julian of Norwich, what it was that nibbled at her ankles.

The next day, the struggle was gone out of me and I felt calm. Sally was by my side and didn't ask questions. I borrowed a book about Julian of Norwich from the library and afterwards, Sally and I went for a walk by the river. I sat under the purple beech tree listening to fish burping in the water while she had a sniff around tree trunks. All around me there was a sense that nature was bursting out of itself. The hands of the chestnut trees were open, shrubs had a hint of moss green running through them and lilac was bubbling with blossom. Something surged in me too and my chest felt very full. I didn't know if it was joy or sorrow but tears spilled out of me. I felt one with the earth and sky and every other living creature. We all breathed the one breath. Even the grass beneath me came alive and I could see the intricate weave of each blade in a way I had never seen before. I sat there for a long while breathing and being breathed, held in the arms of a loving god, my fears dissolving into his large flat chest.

During the weeks that followed, I had no great urge to sort out anything except ensure that Sally's future was secure. People called and brought smiles and heartaches. Others sat like they were waiting to hear my confessions. I knew that the intimacies of my inner world were too fragile for sound. I was in a secret garden nursing new shoots and I didn't know if they would survive.

May arrived and nature was ebullient. I couldn't keep up with the speed of its pulsation. Fresh colours appeared in gardens and hawthorn frothed in ditches. One blossom bowed out and another took its place. Sometimes I felt greedy and wanted to stock up on flowers. I continued to dip into the writings of Julian of Norwich and it opened the door to St John's dark night. There were times when I could do nothing more than feel the contact with the ground and attend to my next breath.

It's early June and I like to be outdoors where I can watch clouds and flight paths, listen to the birds and feel the shawl of The Divine wrap around me in the scented breeze. Today I am in the park. The chestnut trees are in full bloom, their arms outstretched, like torch bearers lighting my way to midsummer.

Letting You Loose

I stand in the field of stubble
above a new road cut through earth
and skirting the city in heavy metal.
This is where I brought you all summer.

You wanted me to play God,
divide the golden sea. You would be
tickled up to your neck in barley,
the child I could not be,
scrunching heads in the palm of your hand,

itching to be close to your father,
a connoisseur of ripe grain,
he stood on the headland reading signs,
waiting for a window of blue that would
save him from a mud brown harvest.

You were frisky in fields of corn,
shaking dry heads as if in a tribal dance,
birds silenced by your altered state,
you stomped the ground,
cleansed the altar for the feast to follow,
and the sad dark of November
when you and I visit our earthly home.
You are on your hunkers stroking silk shoots,
 eyes wide open to the greening of stubble.

Original Blessing

We were labelled as seconds
in the showrooms of seminaries
bargains for the everyday
destined to remain
like oddments on shelves

unless we heard God's whisper
through the cracks and crevices
that we too were fired in the kiln
we too were blessed and broken
like the bread She baked
and offered out to all.

The Rest is Silence

As long as my antennae stretch
outwards there is no silence.
Even in the forest leaves rustle
branches whisper
waves echo in the pine trees.

Here in this room
my ears are aerials
for the hum of fluorescence
pipes purring
murmurs from another room.

When I retreat along the inner path
and come to a clearance
I lay down my load
find the nest already built
hatch out my days.

Phyllida Clarke

I was born in South Africa in 1950, the great-grand-daughter of two dynastic pioneers, thus my life has been shaped within a framework of self-discovery and passionate obsessions.

I am a mother of seven, a teacher, an entrepreneur, a horsewoman, a writer, an artist and a mediator. The author of 'Having it Your Own Way', which explores the options for alternative journeys through childbirth; 'The Straight Forward Method', offering a foolproof way of breaking in horses; 'The Bonjarvey', a novel about one woman's violent metamorphosis from carefree hippy to the powerful maturity of forgiveness.

I am a Bachelor of Science and a Master of Arts but know nothing about science and am a master of nothing. Today I work as peacemaker with the Travelling Community.

Mine is a life grounded in the moment and built around the belief that 'If you will it, so will it be'.

5

Extract from The Bonjarvey
by Phyllida Clarke

Wren Boys

By morning the snow has ceased falling and has set like the frosting on Mrs Foncie's Christmas cake. Kate's breath hovers in clouds before her face. The white framed window panes have ice patterns on the inside. The bed rumbles as the dog growls from deep inside. When she lifts the covers, the dog leaps out, bounds down the stairs and barks hysterically at the kitchen door. Kate pulls a dressing gown over her nightdress and goes down to see what the commotion is all about. Even through thick socks, the flagstones are freezing cold.

Before she opens the door Kate can hear singing outside. For a moment she hesitates but then curiosity gets the better of her. There are three of them hopping about on the doorstep. All are dressed in old clothes, with grass skirts, grass frills below the knees and tall straw hats. Their faces are masked. The singing stops briefly but the drumming on the tight skinned bódhrán keeps going. It's manic, without rhythm, shape or form. The drumstick is flying in all directions. The demented dog barks, howls, yelps and darts at the jiggling feet. He kicks out at her but keeps pounding the drum like a wild thing. The three of them push past the dog, past Kate and surge into the kitchen. The singing starts up again.

Amid the frantic yapping of the dog she can barely make out the words.

> 'We three kings from Bally go far,
> Hungry, cold and needing a jar,
> Don't speak a word, you'll never be heard,
> And you'll never know who we are.'

This is followed by some more verses in Irish and finished off by one of them, who is backing Kate into the room and growling right into her face, with no attempt at tune.

> 'The wren, the wren, the English wren,
> Taste the blood of Irish men.
> We'll deliver a shock,
> With a Fenian cock,
> And maybe then she'll go home again.'

He grabs her arm and spinning her around, thrusts it up between her shoulder blades.

The rim of a cup bites deeply into her cheek as she is pushed, face downwards, over the kitchen table. The cup smashes on the floor.

Her nightdress is being tugged upwards, her thighs crushed against the wood. The drumming is right in her ear. Like a beech log as it splits to the axe, the message is driven home. There's a loud whoop, then suddenly it stops. The drumming stops. The dog is silenced.

'Sweet Jesus! What the hell's that?' The three men gape at the stairwell.

Whatever it is they see there sends them scrambling for the door. They run out, leaving it wide open. Kate opens her mouth to scream. No sound comes. There is nothing in the stairwell but the gloom that is always there. She can taste the blood from her cheek congealing in streaks on her face.

There are pools of melting snow on the flagstones. Kate's socks are wet, the insides of her legs are wet too. She can no longer feel her feet. She looks out into the white farmyard. She sees many footprints all over the place. The scarecrows have fled. She shivers and shuts the door, jamming a chair up against it.

By and by Kate begins to shake uncontrollably. She can't hold the cup of tea, she can't remove her stinking gown. She can't wash the blood from her face. She stares into the fire box and wills it to gather sparks and become a fire. She sits there in the old chair for a long time, squashed into a tight ball of bruised limbs. Numb. Everything rolls over and over in her head. Who was it? What were they on about? What's happened?

These are the same questions her neighbour Marie asks when she finds Kate some hours later, still in her nightdress and smoking a joint.

'Why the hell have you got the chair shoved up agin the door like that?' She forces her way in.

'What the hell's going on here?' Unable to say anything Kate just laughs, with tears bursting the backs of her eyes.

'Oh fuck. This looks bad Kate. You're a mess. Who was it?'

Kate tries to shrug her shoulders but they hurt too much. She pulls hard on the joint and stares into space while the smoke works its way around her lungs. She coughs a few times and pulls again.

Angel of the Road

by *Phyllida Clarke*

The road was beginning to shimmer and dance as the early frost burnt off into a haze of steam. The morning sun, still quite low in the sky, glinted in the dust on my windscreen. Two and a half hours of driving to the airport, half an hour of searching and greeting and an hour of homeward road behind us.

The car was packed with boys. The three in the back were bickering and teasing each other, especially the youngest, a sensitive rather confused lad with speech problems. My fourteen-year-old son was on the passenger seat beside me.

'Why don't you tell them to shut up Mum?'

'Stop boys!'

They kept jibing at their little brother. I tried to distract them by calling into the back.

'Tell us about your trip John, what was the family like?'

'Okay.'

'Okay how?'

'Oh you know, just okay.'

'How did you find the French?'

'They eat a lot and talk too fast.'

'What do they eat?'

'Bread mostly and slimy salami.'

'What's slammy slamy?' The youngest pipes up. The others laugh and mimic him.

'It's a kind of sausage Joe,' I say.

'I love thwthageth.'

'Not these ones you wouldn't, they eat them raw!'

Their words began to blur. My head hummed. My eyes glazed over.

'Mum! Watch the road!' Harry, beside me, shouted.

The next few miles were a struggle, desperately trying to focus and forcing my eyes to stay open. Then it happened. Harry said I went right off the road, up a very steep bank, and miraculously down again. Apparently he caught the wheel and steered the car safely back onto the road. I just remember seeing the tarmac at a peculiar angle and Harry holding the steering wheel. A vehicle whizzed past in the opposite direction with its horn blaring.

I stopped the car. Shaking, I got out. The boys were mute at first and then started shouting and laughing nervously and messing about the way only kids can when they don't know what else to do. Their voices faded behind me as I walked away along the hard shoulder. My life didn't shoot before my eyes, but I knew that I had nearly killed us all, and maybe all those in the other car as well. I breathed deeply drawing in the wonderful smell of life.

For a time I felt I could remember every beat of my thumping heart. A rabbit hopped out in front of me, looked at me as if I was from Mars and then loped away. When my heartbeat was steady I walked back to the car, switched it on and drove carefully home.

Some months later, when I thought they had all forgotten about it, Joe asked me a question.

'Mum, you know that day you dwove off the woad? And you walked off down the werge?'

'Yes, I'll never forget it Joe.'

'Who was the man walking beside you?'

I thought about this for a moment. We never really know what we look like from behind, but just then I had a clear picture in my head of two people walking together. I was on the left and another, a taller figure on my right, was wearing a long coat.

'There wasn't anyone with me Joe.'

'There was Mum, I seen him.'

'How do you know it was a man?' I asked, intrigued.

'He was taller than you and he had a long black coat on.'

Joe is grown up now, a fine handsome married man. I asked him recently about that day.

'Sorry Ma, I can't remember a thing about it.'

The Rise and Fall

A mellow green,
Soft and sweet,
Meadow hay in May.
Searching for the croak of a cricket,
The squeak of a field mouse,
The rise and fall of the breath of life.

A distant moan of traffic blurs the clarity of now.
Where are they all going?
Why don't they stop, listen and hear only the munch of a cudding cow?
What could be so urgent that it's worth drowning the pace of peace with
the longings of the long distance?
The frantic call of the tarmac?

Leave me here,
Let me sink gently in silence.

A Stolen Secret

Sin is the taste of treasure
The smell of cinnamon,
The colour of papal robes.
It feels delicious but makes you late, makes you hate, leaves you empty,
left behind.
Sin is the jam in the doughnut.
It sticks to your clothes, won't wash out,
And as the pleasure fades the taste turns to tin, and burns holes in your
teeth.
It makes wizened parchment out of joyous youth.
Sin is a secret stolen from truth.

Tim Clifford

Mam had to wait three weeks for me. There was no fuss, no hurry, I arrived when I was good and ready. Some things never change. I grew up in Kilkenny, attended college in Limerick then moved to Dublin where I live and work. By day I develop computer software. For fun I pen stories. My dream is to write a book that is read by at least one person I do not know. Chocolate is my weakness, one I happily indulge.

6

Monster Log

by Tim Clifford

Tuesday

If you're reading this, I'm probably dead, or decapitated, or worse. By the way, in case you're wondering, this isn't a diary. It's nothing like that. You won't find love hearts or daisy chains around the picture of some pimple faced wart from fifth class. I'm not like Alice. That's my sap of a sister if you don't know. I'm a boy for a start. My name is Simon, I'm ten, and this is my monster log. About a week ago, I found out something terrible. Something so terrible that it's kind of exciting really. There's a troll living at the end of our garden, just behind the shed, between the fence and the cherry blossom tree, where Dad puts the grass cuttings and potato skins. I haven't actually seen him, but I know he's there. The first clue was the smell. Trolls smell, FACT. Dad says not to be stupid, that it's just the grass decomposing. But he has to be wrong. Nothing smells that bad, except trolls, of course, and maybe Toby Byrne, his uncle makes slurry and he always stinks. When I told Dad this he got angry. He says there's no such thing as trolls and I should forget all about them. He says I should spend more time thinking about homework instead of walking around with my head in the clouds. And he says I should never call anyone smelly, no matter how badly they stink. What does he know? There is a troll in our garden and I'm going to prove it.

Wednesday

For stakeouts you need junk food to stop you from falling asleep. I smuggled a packet of crisps, four chocolate rolls, a can of orange and some biscuits from the kitchen, while Mam was hanging out the washing. I did feel a bit bad leaving her outside, alone, with a troll. It would mess things up a bit if she got eaten. Dad would have to cook the dinner and wash my clothes; he's not very good at either. But, if Mam was eaten, at least that would prove the troll was there. For a stakeout, you also need a good place to hide. Somewhere you can see everything but where no one can see you. The best spot to watch the back garden is from the upstairs bathroom. You can climb up on the toilet and onto the windowsill, if you push Mam's makeup and stuff out of the way. From there you can peep out between the frosted windowpanes. I locked myself in and waited. But I couldn't concentrate, Alice kept knocking on the bathroom door: 'I need to use the toilet, I need to wash my teeth, I need to brush my hair.' If only a troll would eat her; she's so annoying. Why does everyone think girls are nice? They're not. They're sly and mean and devious, and they always get their way. But for once, Mam took my side and told Alice to leave me alone. I knelt there, watching the garden, until my knees were sore and my legs had pins and needles. I was about to give up and go downstairs, when a bird hopped down from one of the trees and started pecking at something deep in the compost heap. It wasn't a very large bird, more of a snack than a meal, but I was sure that the troll would grab it. But nothing happened. Maybe it knew I was watching. I waited another hour, until I'd eaten all my supplies, and then gave up. I tried to climb down, but my legs were like jelly and my foot slipped. It went straight through the toilet seat and got stuck in the bowl. Stupid Alice. She heard the crash and started shouting. Mam had to take the handle off the door just to get in. She went nuts. Alice fell around laughing. Mam told her to stop, that it wasn't funny, but Alice just kept laughing. I screamed at her to shut up but this made Mam angrier. She tried to pull me out but my foot was jammed. When Mam went to call the plumber, Alice decided it would be really funny to try flushing the toilet. The water gushed up over the side and onto the floor. I tried to grab her but I couldn't reach. I shouted at her to get lost but she just stood where I couldn't get her, pulling faces and laughing. It was then that I heard the growl. Trolls growl, FACT. I'm just not sure if it was the troll or Mam.

Thursday

Our dog disappeared last night. Misty was older than I am, and in real years too. Trolls eat dogs, FACT. Especially old ones, the older the better. They like them because they're chewy; I think it's good for their teeth. Also, the bones break up easier and don't get stuck in their throat. Dad left Misty out, just before I went to bed. I told him not to, but he wouldn't listen. 'You've caused enough trouble already today, so don't start that rubbish again,' was all he said. I think he was still mad about the toilet. I saw Misty over near the compost heap, tail between her legs, snarling. She was crouched low, ready to pounce. Then she jumped back and began to bark. She wouldn't stop. Dad came back to the kitchen and banged on the window, complaining that she'd wake the whole neighbourhood. I told him to let her in, that she was scared of the troll. Dad got mad again and sent me upstairs to bed. He never listens to me. He thinks he knows everything. That was the last we saw of Misty. Dad said she must have run away, but I could see he knew better. He just wouldn't admit it.

Friday

Aunt Dolores came for dinner tonight, so I couldn't watch the garden. You can always tell when she's coming because Dad goes quiet and sits in the corner sulking. She's his sister, but they don't get along. She's big and loud and doesn't listen to a word he says. Her hair is brown and bushy, and she wears big, thick glasses. Mam made me take a bath and put on my Sunday trousers and jumper. I don't know why though, Aunt Dolores wears the same grey clothes every time she calls. When she eats, she uses her fingers because the fork isn't big enough. She burps. She farts. She picks her nose and eats it, GROSS. If I did that I'd be in trouble, but no one says a word to her. I think they're all scared. She ate all of her own lasagne and half of mine, and double helpings of dessert. Dad said we should move to the sitting room and have tea by the fire. But Aunt Dolores didn't budge, she was too busy emptying the biscuit tin. She picked up three chocolate digestives and stuffed them into her mouth all at once. Crumbs fell all over the place (she chews with her mouth open). Dad's face turned red and you could almost see steam coming out his ears. It looked like his head would take off any minute. Mam took out a bottle of brandy from the press. Aunt Dolores loves brandy; she'd drink a whole bottle by herself. I don't know why though, it stinks! She smiled and wiped the chocolate from her mouth with the back of her hand. Dad took the bottle and led Aunt Dolores from the kitchen. It's easy to move a mule when you've got a carrot, Mam said, and winked at me. I sat thinking about what she had said. Maybe I needed to try something else if I was going to see my troll. Maybe I needed to find myself a carrot. A very large one. One that the troll couldn't resist.

Saturday

At first I thought about tying Alice to the washing line to see if the troll would take her. But I decided she'd make too much noise, even if I stuffed a sock in her mouth. When Mam and Dad went to bed, I snuck downstairs and got some leftover chicken and a packet of rashers from the fridge. I opened the patio door and walked outside. I held my breath and inched closer and closer to the compost heap. I never took my eyes off it, even when I stood on the garden rake. When I was close enough, I laid a trail back through the garden and inside to the fridge. Then I ran upstairs and waited and waited and waited. My eyes got so heavy I had to pinch myself just to stay awake, but even that didn't work. When I woke I could hear someone below in the kitchen. I grabbed the camera from my bedroom and hurried downstairs. I ran through the door hoping to meet a troll but crashed straight into a tall, skinny man. He had a chicken leg in one hand and was pulling a can of beer from the fridge with the other. His face cracked with an evil grin as he dropped the can and pulled a bread knife from the knife block. Should have stayed in bed boy, he said. I shuffled backwards, then screamed and shouted and picked up things and threw them at him. But it didn't stop him. He came at me until I was right up against the cooker. There was nowhere to go. Just then, a large shadow appeared at the open patio door. It leapt into the kitchen and grabbed the man, lifting him up until they were nose to nose. It growled. The man whimpered and dropped the knife. His mouth opened, though nothing came out. Then he was sent flying through the open door into the garden. Almost without thinking I lifted the camera and it flashed, lighting up the troll's face. He had a really big nose and his face was covered with warts. He wore a pair of old torn jeans. His hair was long and greasy, and he had big yellow eyes. He smiled at me. At least I think it was a smile. I saw his razor sharp teeth and he didn't eat me. Just then I heard someone coming down the stairs and turned to see Dad running into the kitchen. When I looked back around, the troll was gone. Dad shouted a bit about the state of the kitchen, and about what I thought I was doing, but I wasn't really listening. I was thinking about my troll, who had returned to his place behind the shed. Dad picked a careful path through the mess until he stood towering over me. He asked me again what had happened. Nothing, I told him, pushing the camera into my pyjamas' pocket.

Nowhere Else

It's the gentle breath, slow and even. The beating of your heart, seldom heard. The knowledge that there's nowhere I need to be other than where I am.

He Knew

Another black mark. It seemed that everything Patrick did these days was classed a sin. However, this time was different. Deep down he knew what he had done was wrong. He put it from his mind and left the alley, leaving the girl's limp body in a puddle behind him.

Eileen Condon

I was always fond of scribbling and pondering. My parents were friends with writers in Greenwich Village, so I was exposed to lots of creativity. After an adventurous adolescence hitching across America, I ended up teaching English in Manhattan with the late Frank McCourt. Eighteen years ago, I swapped alternate side of the street parking for life on a farm in the Knockmealdown Mountains. This course rekindled a flame for me. I am indebted to my family and friends who encourage me to write. I work in adult education in South Tipperary. When I'm not trying to figure out the meaning of life, and look for ways around its challenges, i.e. if I build a dam, do I get to step in the same river twice?, I enjoy dancing, poetry, playing guitar (thank you God for chords G, C and D) and simple pleasures like a soft boiled egg and a walk on a starry night.

7

Black Olives, Red Shoes

by Eileen Condon

He was the first man to tell her she looked fantastic in red high heels. He watched her from the cushioned chair that most stores provide for bored spouses or loyal but tired friends. Alice caught him staring at her tanned leg and made sure to bend her knee slightly and place her hands on her hips. She did this deftly, instinctively, showing her plumage like an exotic bird whose time has come to find a mate.

His taste was impeccable. The place sold only the most unique Italian leather shoes. She must have passed it often without noticing, a small boutique on Fifth Avenue. It was sandwiched between a shop that sold silk scarves and another that specialised in hand carved tobacco pipes. He had walked her here after work. She was a new employee at the long established Manhattan firm, where he had worked for a few years. He was a good bit older than her and took her under his wing. He confessed it had been lonely there until she came along. Since loneliness was no stranger to her, she felt a certain empathy for the guy. Ah yes, empathy. That was the one trait that always got her into trouble.

'I know he's broke, but he's on the cusp of artistic fame.'

Or,

'I admit he drinks a lot on weekends, but he's so vulnerable when he can't remember where he parked his car.'

Alice's pleas of understanding were a regular source of amusement among her friends. She sat across from one such friend, Louise, in a booth in their favourite diner.

'He walks me to the subway after work. He's so attentive.' Alice launched her new defence while drawing watery images with her finger on the inside of the steamed up window.

Louise smeared cream cheese over her poppy seed bagel and rolled her eyes at Alice.

'Hey Louise, don't give me that look.'

'Come on Alice, I could write the script by now.'

'Not this time. Malcolm's so....'

'Whoa. Let me guess. Different?'

'How'd you know?'

Immediately, Alice got the 'Louise look.' The Louise look says 'Duh' without having to say 'Duh.'

'I'm just wondering,' her friend said between bites, 'how does all this fit in with that other man in your life? You know, your husband.'

Alice went quiet and looked at the crumbs on her friend's plate. The shaking of her knee under the table made the poppy seeds collide with each other in a miniature game of pinball. She didn't want this sharp reminder about Matthew. It was Sunday. If she were at home, she'd be helping him look for his car.

Malcolm was the first man to educate Alice about spoon back chairs. She watched his well groomed hand slide up and over the arch of the chair's mahogany frame. He rubbed his thumb into the polished wood in a circular motion, like he was giving its back a massage and working out a knot of tension in its shoulder.

'See how the back is bent in the shape of a spoon? The hollow in the middle makes it valuable,' he told her.

She never knew this. He loved antiques and they spent many afternoons browsing in different shops. Alice was impressed by his knowledge. Afterwards, she found herself looking for telltale signs of worth in furniture: curved backs, curved legs, curved feet. She liked the feeling of knowing things others didn't know. With Malcolm, she had crossed a divide and climbed onto a ledge. Yes, she felt elevated.

As time went on, she longed for five o'clock on Fridays. That's when she and Malcolm did things together. Marriage to Matthew had come to mean lonely weekends. She was in no rush to get home. Malcolm was more particular about his choice of drink. He liked extra dry Grey Goose Vodka martinis, shaken not stirred. They sometimes stopped in a classy place near Central Park, where male staff moved fluidly behind the bar and called her 'Madam'. She thought of Matthew planted on a stool in a

Blarney Rose bar somewhere, listening to Rod Stewart's Greatest Hits. At first, she had been flattered that Matthew wanted her. It was his recklessness and disregard for authority that had first attracted her. But now, under the harsh fluorescent of matrimony, his irresistible quirks had become exasperating imperfections. Her failure at domesticating her husband baffled Alice. She believed that men like Matthew drifted through the world until the right woman came along who would take on the role of saviour. Alice had been up for the job. She fantasised about his being grateful to her for taming him and pictured other women being jealous of her secret ingredient. But things were not going her way. Gratitude was not what she was experiencing from Matthew.

With Malcolm, she found a new reason to feel special. Here was another man who chose her above all others. He appreciated her. She felt like one of those drone bees she read about in National Geographic. In order to pick a mate, the queen bee gradually increases her altitude as she flies. Each time she climbs a bit higher, she loses more male drones who can't keep up. Eventually, there are only a few left. The queen mates with these drones because they have shown themselves to be superior to the other contenders. In a twist of gender, Alice felt like she was selected by Malcolm, the queen. He sought her out in the staff room. He wanted her to walk him to his office and liked the commotion this caused.

'He's just using you.' Alice was shocked by the snide remark of Barbara, a co-worker.

Poor Barbara, she thought. I guess it's hard being forty and single in a city where the ratio of women to men is two to one. If she were honest, Alice relished Barbara's jealousy. It was further confirmation that she possessed the unique formula other women lacked.

Valentine's Day fell on a Friday. Alice was delighted. She and Malcolm were going for supper after browsing in Bloomingdale's. She had acquired a taste for espresso and olives, though not together. It was all thanks to Malcolm. He was in great form as they strolled side by side up Fifth Avenue. He had applied for an in-house promotion and got it. Obviously, he wanted to celebrate with her. She tried hard to forget the last outburst from Louise.

'You're spending Valentine's Day with Malcolm? What kind of a snake are you?'

Alice was seriously considering scratching Louise's name off her 'best friend' list. She wanted someone to mirror her justification, not challenge her lack of integrity.

The waiter assumed that they were a couple and showed them to a quiet table. Alice smiled frequently across at Malcolm. He avoided her gaze, staring at the back of a spoon. Examining the sterling mark no doubt, she thought. Eventually, he broke the silence.

'Bob's thrilled about the promotion,' he said tentatively. 'We're going to Martha's Vineyard for the weekend to celebrate.'

On their frequent walks through the city, Malcolm often spoke of his flatmate Bob. Alice's face fell. She was crushed that he preferred his stupid flatmate to her. Reading her features, Malcolm continued guiltily.

'Alice, you know that I'm...well...you know.'

She looked at him puzzled at first, and then immediately processed what he was saying. There had been signs: his meticulous attention to grooming, his love of women's fashion, his extensive colour vocabulary, even his use of her to get a promotion? No, she didn't know. How could she not know? Oh God. She was not looking forward to her next cup of coffee with Louise.

'Yes, of course I know.' She spoke light heartedly, as the waiter brought the bread.

She could feel Malcolm's relief. He continued to chat about this and that. She focused on the perfectly formed balls of butter in the dish on the table and flattened them one by one with her fish knife.

It was late when she walked up three flights of stairs to her apartment. She was startled when she saw Matthew. He was asleep on the couch in a wrinkled but clean shirt. He was wearing his good shoes, the ones he had worn when they married several years before. His strong limbs were at ease, his arms outstretched, trusting and open. As she stood there, looking at him, Alice thought of how much she had changed. Her free and easy nature had worn away, leaving behind a hardness like an olive pit. Spotting Matthew's flaws, rather than admitting her own, had become a convenient hobby. At some point, she began confusing their marriage licence with a sculptor's licence, which she used vigorously to shape and mould him. Every time Matthew did something that clashed with her idea of who he should be, she hacked off another corner, using a chisel of shame. Who he was had stopped being enough for her. She had become the queen bee and Matthew, the useless drone.

Outside their apartment window, a cavalcade of sirens on their way to someone else's mess broke through the silence in the room. Matthew stirred from his sleep.

'Hey stranger.' He spoke in a deep voice. He looked tired, but he was sober.

Alice went over and sat next to him on the couch. She allowed her right thigh to brush against his left one for a second before moving her legs back together. They had not been intimate for a while. Even though she missed his touch, she had fostered a distance between them that was now more comfortable than the risk of physical closeness. It was hard to tell whether he was disappointed or relieved. She kicked off her red high heels.

'Cool shoes,' he said.

'Thanks. They're killing me. Funny how things that look nice can hurt so much.'

'I'm gonna order a pizza for Valentine's Day. Want black olives on it? You seem to like those lately.'

She was surprised he had noticed. It had been a long time since their fridge was stocked with ingredients for shared meals.

'You know, come to think of it,' she said, 'I prefer pepperoni.'

Unexpected Guests

As Suzanne instructs us to write about silence, I am conscious of my sniffles. I've sniffled twice. I'm trying not to do it again. I rustle papers, my breathing is shallow. I gather myself and wait. There, that's better. Now other people's breathing is louder than mine. The hum of the heat in the pipes overhead is magnified. At other times, like when I'm sitting next to Rachel and asking her where she bought her shoes, I don't hear it at all. Silence lets my thoughts step up from the dark backstage of my mind into the floodlights, where I sit in the audience deciding if I'm going to cast them for this piece.

Recently, I have come to honour and respect silence. I have also been familiar with its dread and my compulsion to pollute it with senseless drivel, just to quash it, to drown out its unnerving presence. Now, I try to be tolerant and open to the unexpected guests that silence brings. I'm less worried about whether I'm going to like them. Instead, I let them speak while I do my best to sit and stay quiet and hear what they have to say.

A Woman of Seven Sins

Mrs O'Halloran loved it when it came time to judge the best apple tart. She knew that when it came to pastry, there was no woman in the parish better with a rolling pin. In fact, as her neighbours laid out their tarts on the trestle tables in the marquee, she didn't even salute them. Oh no, Betty O'Halloran was way too proud! First prize was a weekend away in Donegal. Even though she and Jim owned an entire holiday home complex in Cahirciveen, that didn't matter, she still wanted more.

As final preparations were made for the judging, Betty noticed that Madge Ryan's tart looked a lot better than other years. This worried her. Envy coursed through her clogged arteries as best it could. When the ladies were called outside for a group photo, Mrs O'Halloran stayed behind in the marquee. Then, she started eating. She ate her way up one trestle table and down the other, stuffing herself with tart. The juice dribbled out the sides of her mouth. She was fuelled by a mighty wrath. Any tarts she couldn't eat, she piled high and flung like frisbees into the nearby field, where all breeds of dogs waited to be paraded. Lucky for them, tart was on the menu.

When it came time to judge the contest, only one apple tart was left. Mrs O'Halloran got the blue ribbon. She and Jim went off to Donegal. While they were there, she lusted after seven local fishermen. She named each one by the days of the week. Tonight it was Wednesday's turn.

Mrs O'Halloran ended her days in disrepute. Jim left her for Madge Ryan, she was banned from entering any more apple tart competitions, and she was completely friendless. Those who had compassion tried to get her to rejoin the human race. She thought about it now and then, once every five years to be precise, but in the end, she never bothered her arse.

Jane de Montmorency

Born in Dublin many years ago I grew up with a foot on either side of the Irish Sea. Home in Co. Kilkenny, school in the UK. Life in swinging sixties London creating perfumes for a top cosmetic house was followed in 1967 returning to live in Blessington, Co. Wicklow. Later with three children to educate I progressed through a number of diverse jobs, Montessori school administrator, farm secretary and craft shop owner. Since returning to live in Kilkenny thirty years ago I've travelled to every corner of Ireland marketing Irish crafts. On retirement I studied for the B.A. in Local Studies provided here in Kilkenny by NUIM and being an eternal student have now taken the course in Creative Writing. Hopefully all my previous experiences will give me plenty of material to use.

8

Returning Home

by Jane de Montmorency

My bedroom is dark and silent. The door is closed for the first time in many months, there is no longer any need to leave it open. The darkness is intense. My warm bed has a womblike quality. In it I am snug and safe from the outside world. Now is a time for reflection, today is different, I must decide my future. This is a defining moment for me and I am trying to think positively.

This is the bedroom I had as a child in this old house which stands amidst tall trees, surrounded by stone walled fields stretching towards the distant hills. My parents moved here when my father left the army after the war, a war about which he rarely spoke. He was a writer, a poet, a dreamer. My mother, a music teacher, was the dynamo that powered our family. It was she who was involved in the local community, travelling each day to teach in the girls' school in the nearby town, training the church choir and organising the annual music festival.

I was a happy and carefree child growing up with my two younger brothers, until something changed during my teenage years. Life wasn't offering me enough, boredom set in. I became rebellious and difficult. Amidst cries of 'You don't understand me' and 'There's nothing to do here' I left for college. I think my parents breathed a sigh of relief. I was delighted to go, a whole new world opened up. I became an urban creature revelling in the noise, the lights, the excitement and stimulation of city life.

I shortened my name to Lindy. Belinda Barrett didn't suit my new persona at all. Dull, dull, dull. Lindy was the new, vital me who joined every club, embraced every new cause and lived life to the full. After college I never looked back; my career in marketing forged ahead. I travelled the world, I had a flat in London and later a loft in New York.

I kept in touch of course, visiting occasionally; the obligatory trips home for Christmas every few years and for my brothers' weddings. They both married nice, but rather uninspiring girls and settled in a town about 20 miles away. I avoided coming home for the christenings of the children which inevitably followed. My mother's letters, she wrote to me weekly throughout her life, were filled with their activities.

'Susie has her first tooth. Mark scored a goal last Saturday' and so on. She clearly doted on her grandchildren. No babies for me though; no marriage either – it would cramp my style. I replied far less frequently.

When I heard of my mother's accident I was devastated. Driving home from work on a wet winter's evening five years ago her car was hit by a speeding van, ending upside down in the ditch. She died before the ambulance arrived. I flew home immediately for her funeral. It was an emotional time for all of us, recollections of good times and bad were interspersed with debates on what we could plan for the future. My father was much feebler than I had realised. He was of course approaching his eightieth birthday. When we saw how helpless he was it was presumed that I would give up my career and return to look after him in his declining years. Neither of my sisters in law seemed prepared to help. Both had young children to care for of course and they either couldn't or wouldn't make the time.

'It won't be for long' one of my brothers had said, rather callously, I thought. 'He's not at all well himself you know. Why don't you take a career break for a year or so and then we can see how it goes.'

I wondered what had been going on between them through all those years.

It wasn't always easy of course. My father missed my mother dreadfully. He had depended on her for so much and I was a poor substitute. At first he spoke little and seemed wrapped in his own world; he had periods of depression and self-pity.

'I'm nothing but a burden to you my dear,' he would say. 'The sooner I go the better.'

Often the silence was oppressive but gradually a strong bond began to develop between us. Once again I became Belinda, he never called me Lindy. In caring for him I discovered much about myself and absorbed some of his points of view which I came to appreciate. My own loss and the feeling I had that I had missed so much by not knowing my mother better, together with regrets for things undone, visits not made, conversations unfinished, all coloured my decision to remain at home.

Perhaps also I was disillusioned with my own life. I found it a relief to be off the career treadmill. Had I really been happy in such an ambition fuelled environment? As time passed I became used to the slower pace of country life, it began to suit me. I adapted to living with the seasonal changes and to the complexities of rural life and the difficulties of running this old fashioned house. The large rooms made it difficult to heat. I seemed to be always carrying in winter logs. The long passages and steep staircase were tiring and yet I've grown to appreciate its charm. With all the new technology available I was able to run my business from the house for a while and then it palled on me. I was too far away from the coalface. I closed it down apart from some advisory work.

To be truthful I must also confess to many moments of frustration and resentment. My brothers only visited occasionally, pleading family commitments as an excuse. Fair enough I suppose, in their eyes I'd had my freedom for years. My father had also made it clear to them that the house would be mine when his time came. This now is the core of my dilemma. Should I stay? I've become very happy here. Or should I strike out again on some new path? If I am to leave here I must explore some new area to work in but I feel it would be difficult to re-enter the rat race. Now when I need to force myself to make a decision I realise how much I have reconnected with the place where I was born, grew up in and eventually fled from.

My older more mature self baulks at the idea of uprooting and moving on again. Moving to where anyway? At first, plucked from an intensely urban lifestyle and used to what I thought of as all the conveniences of city life, I found the silence and isolation hard to bear. My opportunities to get out and about have been restricted by the time I could spend away from tending my father as he became increasingly fragile. Trips further than to the local town have been rare. I am blessed that Mrs G, who had helped my mother, still comes three mornings a week and so I can rush out to shop; have my hair done, I like to keep my appearance up; and go to the library. She brings a load of gossip with her as well and doubtless regales her other 'houses' with news of us. Not that there is much to tell. Some afternoons our neighbour Robert came to play chess with my father. They had many interests in common and enjoyed each other's company. A kind, intelligent man, now a widower he often brought a book or other small thoughtful gift.

I should have kept more in touch with my family over the intervening years but time seemed to slip by. I hadn't really allowed for the fact that they were changing also, growing up, growing older. It was a shock to find so much altered when I returned. Somehow I had expected life here to have been preserved as if in a bubble. Yet it was different, much had changed. I remembered how beautifully kept the garden had been. My mother loved her herbaceous border and the rose garden and my father had worked away growing vegetables and fruit. He said he got most of the inspiration for his writing when out there weeding, digging and hoeing. Now it was all sadly over grown. I try to put some order on it and, like him, have come to enjoy the time I spend doing so. Last summer he enjoyed the days he could sit out in his wheelchair and proffer advice.

One thing that remained the same was his collection of books crowding the shelves in every room. It was a great delight to me, as a child, that he read to me each bedtime. Now that our roles are reversed I have been able to repay him. I read to him for many hours appreciating this pleasure we share. Our time became our own, especially over this last difficult winter. I left my door ajar in case he woke in the night then I would read to him until he settled again. Poetry, Wordsworth especially was a particular favourite during those quiet, still hours. Music became another shared passion. My interest and appreciation was reawakened by the extensive collection of records in the house; I tentatively started to play the piano again, a skill I had not practised for many years. Although I knew I would never be able to replace my mother, we both gained many hours of pleasure.

My father lies in his room at the top of the stairs. He died two nights ago. They came and laid him out in the morning. There have been visitors to the house all day. Some were people who had never bothered to call once in his last lonely years.They said all the conventional things.

'I'm sorry for your trouble.'

'He was a kind man, God bless him.'

And some asked:

'What are you going to do now? Will you stay on?'

A good question. Will I stay on? Do I want to live amongst these people? Will I be happy? Probably, as happy here as anywhere else. Where else would I go anyway? The threads of my former life are broken.

A mixture of emotions overwhelms and surprises me. Sadness of course; relief for him that his pain is over; a sense of loss for there will never again be anyone so dependent upon me and finally, apprehension for myself in the future. It will be quiet and quite lonely if I stay. I shall miss his presence. I think we had grown together in quite a special way over the last few years. To my surprise, I discovered in myself much of the caring attitude I might have lavished on a child if I'd had one.

I wonder if any of the neighbours will call? There are few enough who did. Will Robert still come? I'm no good at chess, perhaps he will have time to teach me. The dawn light is starting to seep into the room around the edge of the curtains as I make up my mind. I cannot bring myself to leave. If I belong anywhere it is here.

Nora Farrell

I worked as a library assistant, teacher and mother and enjoy yoga and line dancing. The tastiest hot dog I ever ate was bought for me by a stranger near the Eiffel Tower on a day when all my money was gone. My entry in the Kilkenny People short story competition 'The Concert' was a winner.

Growing up in Dublin was fun, our gang walked on Dollymount Strand, made holes in the sand and watched them fill with water, laughed when dogs barked at seagulls and had our hideout in St. Anne's Park. We played queenie-i-o, giant steps and piggy beds. Now I walk along the Nore, stroll in Castle Park and only play when no one is watching.

9

Identity

by Nora Farrell

Stacey looked tiny and determined as she ran and seated herself at a table where two boys and a girl were already colouring. She didn't even glance at me as I left. Her teacher told me this was a good thing, a sign that Stacey felt secure. Obviously my daughter was dealing with her first day in school better than I was.

I walked home in my pink tracksuit. It was the best of my casual wear and warm. I arrived on our street, feeling weepy, to see an elegant woman in her forties locking the door of a white Audi. She was dressed as I used to be; a navy jacket and skirt, snow white blouse, navy high heels and a matching handbag. Her hair was wavy and highlighted. A removal van pulled up seconds later. She had entered the house before I got a chance to shout hello.

In that first week I adjusted to packing lunch for Stacey, strapping three-year-old Robbie into the pushchair and walking to the school gates. I caught glimpses of my neighbour. She came and went at odd hours, was always impeccably dressed and looking confident. The more I saw of her the more self-conscious I became. How had I managed to let myself go? My hair was long and tied back. I hadn't been to a hairdresser in months. My clothes were bought for comfort and apart from lip balm I'd forgotten what make up was. My business suits hung in the wardrobe, all a size too small and years out of date.

I had returned enthusiastically to the office when Stacey was three months old. Office politics seemed dull. My daughter had quietly taken over my heart. I longed for her warm body, baby smell, gurgles and smiles. At six months she sat up and I wasn't there. No career breaks were available so I resigned.

'Whose turn is it to drop Stacey off?' Bill had joked the first morning I stayed home. I laughed, standing in my dressing gown, our daughter in my arms. Bill leaned over and kissed my cheek and the top of Stacey's head. 'The trip to work will be a breeze for me now,' he said as he left.

I missed the second car. Bill and I both missed foreign holidays and weekends away. But watching Stacey as she tried to burst bubbles in the bath or staring at her long dark eyelashes as she slept gave me more joy than any job.

Two years later Robbie was born. When he sat up I was there. When he began throwing his toys out of the pram Stacey threw them back in. They both laughed out loud.

'Our children are learning to play,' I said that evening. Resigning had seemed worth it. Now I wondered had I lost myself in the process?

Bill discovered the man next door was called Hugh Talbot, loved cars and was a member of the local Yacht Club.

'He told me they'll be having parties most Fridays,' Bill said, 'and for a minute I thought he'd invite us but he was only worried about the noise. If it's too much for us we're to let him know.'

I shrugged, so much for friendly neighbours.

As soon as the guests began to arrive Bill found excuses to go outside. He pulled up weeds, fiddled with the engine of his car or strolled slowly around the garden.

'Wow,' he said coming in. 'Did you see the getup of those women? The one in red had the lowest cut top I've ever seen.'

That comment made me think of getting a makeover, or going to the library and actually reading something other than nursery rhymes or the Mr Men series which was Stacey's favourite. But somehow the two hours I had to myself when Robbie was at playschool disappeared and the rest of the day the children absorbed my attention.

Our neighbours remained distant. Mr Talbot was polite but his wife never spoke.

I was alone in the house when I noticed her step from the Audi holding a bag of groceries. She slipped. Cornflakes, rashers and oranges spilled onto the pavement. I was amazed at the ordinariness of her purchases. Because she was making no effort to stand I went out reluctantly and offered my assistance. She took my hand and pulled herself up.

'Do you spend your whole life looking out your window?' she snarled.

'Can a person not even slip in peace?'

I was flabbergasted and stamped home. I picked up the phone with a shaking hand and called my mother.

'I'm fit to strangle your one next door.' I began as soon as she picked up.

'That's not like you. What happened?'

'I helped her up when she slipped and she yelled at me instead of saying thanks.'

'Poor you.' I could hear suppressed merriment in my mother's voice. 'I'm sure she looked like a right sight.'

'She sure did, sitting on the ground in her designer gear, a ladder in her tights and oranges rolling everywhere.'

Mam laughed. 'I'd say she was embarrassed. Wouldn't you be?'

I had to agree. 'You should have seen her face. It was beetroot.'

'There you are then. There was nothing personal about her attack.'

My mother is one of those people who insist on seeing the best in everybody.

'But she's been so standoffish,' I said, 'anytime I smile at her she pretends not to see.'

'Maybe she's just shy. I've got to go love; I'm off to a coffee morning.'

I put the phone down wondering if I'd got things all wrong.

Robbie and I were kicking a ball around the back garden the next afternoon when I heard sobbing. I stood on my tippy toes and peered into Talbot's. Water sprayed from a snake stone fountain, terracotta pots overflowed with pansies and paving stones led to the decking where Mrs Talbot huddled. An umbrella shaded her face.

'I'm putting on the kettle now if you'd like to come in for tea,' I shouted impulsively.

'I'd love to,' she replied in a gentle voice, startling me.

She arrived without bothering to repair her makeup. There were shadows under her eyes and her lashes were wet.

'Hugh doesn't encourage me to have friends; that's why I've been distant, but I'm sincerely sorry for yesterday. I'm Andrea, by the way.'

'Cynthia,' I answered, shaking hands.

'I'm upset because …' Tears threatened and I pushed the box of tissues across the kitchen table.

'You don't have to explain,' I said.

'It's all right, I'd like to,' she answered, wiping her eyes. 'My daughter hasn't been speaking to me for months. She says I let Hugh walk all over me; and now my marriage itself is at a crossroads.'

'How awful,' I said. 'Are you married long?'

'Twenty-two years. The reception was in the Shelbourne and we honeymooned in Barbados.'

'You must be worth a fortune now if you could afford that then,' I exclaimed before I could stop myself.

Andrea gave a watery laugh and clutched the mug of tea I placed in front of her.

'He was my boss. I really looked up to him, you know? The suave older man. He took me to fancy restaurants and taught me to sail on his own boat. I couldn't believe my luck. When he drove up to our terraced house in his Mercedes, well …' Andrea rolled her eyes. 'The neighbours talked about him for days and my parents were more proud of my ability to attract him than of my typing skills.'

I smiled at her and glanced out at Stacey and Robbie playing in the garden.

'I can't go on like this,' she said. 'We've never been equals, Hugh and I. He sees me as a trophy not a person. You're so confident Cynthia, not needing makeup and wearing clothes for comfort.'

'That's one way of looking at it,' I answered, 'But you look so classy. I've wanted to dress up since you moved in.'

'Really?'

'Yes,' I nodded. 'I've been afraid of becoming mammy and not being Cynthia anymore.'

'I know exactly what you mean. I've played at being Mrs Talbot so well my younger self wouldn't recognise me,' she laughed.

I noticed a light drizzle falling and stood up to call the children.

'You must be doing something right,' I said, over my shoulder. 'Your parties sound like fun.'

'I hate them. They're for Hugh's business associates. All he thinks about is work.'

The children ran in shaking raindrops from their hair.

'Chocolate bikkies, great, can I have one?' Stacey asked.

'Me too, me too,' Robbie said.

We were still talking when the biscuits were gone and the tea cold.

Stacey made tea for her teddies and Robbie drew with his chunky crayons.

We discovered we had a lot in common. Both of us were afraid of losing ourselves for different reasons.

Mrs Talbot looked like a much nicer person when she left clutching a picture Robbie had done for her. Her smile was more effective than any makeup.

Not Today

by Nora Farrell

The door was open when he arrived home from school that day. He tightened his grip on his bag and ran into the hall. 'Feck it,' he heard his father yell.

Tommy was immobilised. Bad words were forbidden. Last week he said 'Christ' by mistake and his father walloped him across the left ear. He wanted to call his mother now but his voice stuck in his throat. His heart was pounding. Loud sobs began echoing down the stairs, then the next door neighbour appeared out of Tommy's own sitting room, put her hand on his shoulder and said:

'Come home with me now. No cause for you to be going upstairs.'

'Wha... What's wrong?'

Mrs Murphy pretended she hadn't heard. He dropped his schoolbag and allowed her lead him down the path. A car screeched to a halt as they reached the gate. His aunt jumped out. Jan had a merry laugh, drove a cool car and kicked ball as well as any man. She wasn't laughing now.

'Into the car with you,' she said, holding the door open.

Tommy looked at Mrs Murphy.

'It's OK love, go with your Auntie.'

He climbed into the back seat. The leather was cold under his skin.

'Where's Mammy?'

Aunt Jan revved the engine and drove off.

'Why's Daddy home in the middle of the day?'

'I can't talk when I'm driving.'

Tommy knew this was untrue. The last day they'd been out they'd sung Old MacDonald all the way home from the picnic.

Cousin Peter, who was eight, three years older than Tommy, let him win at marbles and hardly spoke at all. It wasn't much fun winning when he didn't have to try. At dinner they sat eating fish fingers, beans and potatoes in the kitchen and when Tommy asked Jan to play ball she said she was too busy.

'What's wrong?' he asked again.

'Let's play snap,' Uncle Dennis said, placing a pack of cards on the table.

Aunt Jan gave him a pair of Peter's pyjamas. She had to roll up the bottoms of the legs and the cuffs on the arms. Both boys drank warm milk and then Tommy lay down in the pullout bed beside Peter's. This room was darker and smaller than his room at home. He missed his toy soldiers on his bedside locker.

Later, when he couldn't sleep, he went downstairs for water.

'The police arrived about fifteen minutes after you left,' he heard Uncle Dennis say.

'Thank God the poor child didn't see anything he shouldn't have,' Aunt Jan answered.

When he pushed open the door he knew by their faces not to ask questions. Why had the police been at his house? Maybe because his father said bad words. Daddy had often told Tommy that they could get him into trouble.

The next morning Peter was told to get dressed for school but Tommy was let stay in Peter's pyjamas. He ate his cereal quietly sitting on the wooden chair at the table, swinging his legs and looking around him.

'I'll drop Peter off,' Uncle Dennis said. He ruffled Tommy's hair on his way out. Aunt Jan nodded and then sat opposite Tommy. She had tea in a white mug with a black J on it. Mammy taught Tommy the alphabet before he started school. He knew all the letters to see and was able to write his own name. Aunt Jan's eyes were darker than usual and the belt on her dressing gown was pulled tight around her middle. She looked fat.

'You look fat,' he said, and then wondered if he had been rude. Big people wanted to hear the truth about some things but not others. Aunt Jan laughed. Tommy laughed too; he must have got it right. Then Jan laughed so much she began to cry. Big tears rolled down her cheeks.

Tommy was scared. He'd never heard big people cry before. Yesterday it was Daddy, today it was Jan.

'What's wrong?' he asked, climbing down from his chair and going to hers. She pulled him onto her lap and he was surprised when she answered.

'There's been an accident.'

She rubbed his head and he could smell her minty breath.

'What accident?'

'Your Mammy fell.'

'Is that why Daddy was at home?'

She pushed him out to the edge of her lap and looked at him.

'Yes love, it is.'

'And why he was saying bad words?'

She nodded. 'Your Daddy was upset.'

'Is Mammy better now?'

'She's at the hospital.'

'Can I go see her?'

'Not yet. We have to see how it goes.'

'Why did the police come?'

'The police?' Aunt Jan looked startled. Then she placed him on the floor and began walking upstairs. 'We'll give you a nice warm bath now. The police like to know about accidents, that's why they came.'

'And I don't have to go to school?'

'Not today.'

Hear the Soul

Greyness knocking on the window of a room in semi darkness. The weight of unspoken thoughts filling the air, rustling paper, the click of a pen, movement of a shoe. Silence allows me hear my soul speak.

Only One Sin

Sins are what I was warned against as a child – a sliding scale of 'Thou shalt nots' leading to the agonising fire of hell.

For me now there is only one sin – lack of respect for my own wonderfulness and the wonderfulness of others.

Majella Gorman

I live outside Thurles with my husband John and two children. A firm believer that there is much to see, do and learn my travels have taken me to Japan, America, and Europe. A positive outlook combined with a love of nature and the outdoors helps to keep me grounded. For the past decade family life has been at the core of my being where I have embraced the gift of motherhood. A love of books and a passion for words has led me down the writing path. I have allowed myself to hear the whispers of my soul and given life to my creative dreams.

10

A New Way

by Majella Gorman

A restless heart
disentangling the day's activities,
stealing sleep, stealing peace.
Shattered dreams come to the fore.
Hope is on the peripheral.

I close my eyes and settle within,
a longingness overcomes me.
I grapple with thoughts, haunted by images,
violated by ruminations,
I wish to cry out, no more.

I breathe again, steady and even,
thoughts keeled over, banished for ever.
I wriggle with freedom.
Peace is euphoric, tranquillity a gift.
I am enveloped by the light.
There is a new brightness, a new way.

Journey

by Majella Gorman

Ellie fingered the locket around her neck, which was feeling more like a stone with each passing day. She unclasped the chain, held it in her hand. Inside the black and white image of herself and her mother smiled back at her. A gift for her twenty-first birthday, together forever read the inscription. That was a decade ago, a time when life had been carefree.

She placed the locket on the table, picked up the phone. Her fingers defied her; unable to punch out the numbers. She looked at her hands and then around the studio. The clay on the wheel begging for attention, the plates set out for painting. She ran her fingers through her short black spiky hair playing the conversation with her mother over and over again. How could she have kept it from her? During her school days she had listened to her friends grumble about their mothers not understanding them. Not Ellie though. She had felt secure. Now doubts filled her mind, lines of reality became blurred. She picked up the car keys and banged the door on her way out.

Rose was sitting at the kitchen table, the tea in front of her growing colder. How could she explain decisions made a lifetime ago? She had tried so hard not to let her pain filter through to Ellie. Sometimes, when she looked at her daughter, it was Jim's essence that came alive. Her Jim, who died when their daughter was six months old. Her Jim, who teased her so many times that she was ruled by her heart and not by her head, when decisions had to be made. But she found his heart, knew that she and Ellie held a special place there.

Disturbed from her thoughts by the familiar sound of Ellie's car, she moved to the back door and opened it, looked at her daughter's pale face; eyes that should be alive and sparkling, now deep with darkness.

'It's so good to see you.' Rose let Ellie in.

'Had to come.'

She watched her daughter's lips tighten, the lower lip disappearing under clenched teeth.

'I hate when we argue, sit down,' and placed a cup in front of her.

'I can't believe you didn't tell me sooner.'

'I'd meant to, never seemed to be the right time. Maybe I, maybe I chose to be silent, I don't know.'

'You chose to be silent…My grandfather left us his cottage and you

80

sit here and say you chose to be silent!'

'It was a long time ago. I saw it like an insurance policy. There if we needed it.'

'We never got holidays. We could have had one.'

'I was never going to spend a night there. Your father didn't even want to be buried in his home town. Said he felt alive where we were.'

Rose let her mind drift to happy moments in her home. The Jim she had known and loved was in her red brick house, where they had set out together full of hopes and dreams. No treasured memories were to be found for him in the country. Jim's heart was in the city where the warmth of his life unfolded. He didn't believe in going back. She remembered the pain of loss, the struggle to fulfil his wishes when he died, the opposition that she had met. Three months later Jim's own father died of a heart attack and she recalled the numbness of travelling to the funeral. Feeling all eyes upon her, the outsider in the gathering.

Ellie watched her mother move her fingers over her wedding band, touching and caressing it.

'Go on,' she encouraged her mother.

'I got a letter in the post saying the cottage was ours.'

'You must have got a shock.'

'I was grieving for your father, taking care of you. There was a neighbour, a man called Jack Daly, kept the place maintained for me.'

'What's it like now?'

'You can go and see for yourself.' Rose stood up and took an envelope from the press, handed it to Ellie.

'The key's in it, the directions and Jack Daly's phone number if you run into difficulties.'

Ellie held the envelope and felt the key through the thin paper.

'Will you come with me?'

'No, this isn't about me, it's about you, this is your time.'

Rose stood at the window watching Ellie's car move away. Had she been right? Should she have told her earlier? It was just the two of them for so long. But she saw it in Ellie now, that same restlessness that her father had. This should be the happiest time in her daughter's life, yet there was an unease surrounding her. She had to let her go and trust. Rose placed her hand on her chest and felt a familiar pain rise. Moved to the sofa, eased her weary self down. She looked at the photo of her husband.

'Jim you had so little time, but I've been given time, time to sort out the details.'

Ellie will understand, come round. Rose picked up the notebook beside her. Only two items left on her list; to ring Jack Daly, and to return Dr Fitzmaurice's call.

Ellie paced the small studio eyeing the envelope on the table. She had to go, had to see what it was like. Took the key out of the envelope and felt the metal brush against her skin. This was the key to her father's home, where he lived and was raised for sixteen years. Ellie remembered nights sitting beside her mother, the wedding album on her lap, turning the pages and loving it. As a child she had asked so many questions about her father. What colour eyes had he? What music had he liked? She had heard the story of how her grandfather died within months of her father. How could she have not known about the cottage? She placed the key in her pocket, the envelope in her bag.

The roads began to narrow and she left the traffic behind. Her hands tightened on the steering wheel as she saw the first signpost for Lissy village. She knew the house was just outside the village. Slowing down she approached her destination, peering forward trying to absorb it all, her eyes fell on the cottage. It was exactly as the description had read: white cottage, navy door flagged by windows on either side. She parked the car and sat for a moment. The timber fence with a wild rose bush sprawling through it at one end, a garden seat placed under the left window. She opened the small timber gate, walked up towards the door. Her breath quickening, she placed the key in the door and felt the lock release, pushed the door inwards. A small living room revealed itself. An open fireplace with porcelain dogs upon the mantlepiece. She walked under an archway which led to a small kitchen. A square table stood in the centre of the room, covered by an oilcloth, an empty vase on top. She moved to the presses, opened and closed them, circled the room. Picked up the vase from the table and stood beside the window, turning it in her hands. What had she expected? A trace of life that had disappeared thirty years ago? As a child, had her father played in this backyard, ran in and out of this room? So many questions, unknown questions that she was seeking answers to.

Startled from her thoughts by the sound of a knock on the door and movement in the hallway, she placed the vase back and headed out.

'You must be Ellie, Jack Daly is the name.' He extended his hand. 'Your mother rang to say you were calling.'

Ellie looked at the weather beaten man in front of her as she took his hand.

'My mother tells me you take care of this place.'

'I pass this way every day on my walks with Ruffles, 'tis easy for me to pop in.'

'It's all so… so clean.'

'We haven't had anyone staying for a while.'

'Oh! It's rented out.'

'No, no, just when someone needs a roof in an emergency. If there was a funeral or a wedding in the village, one of the neighbour's relatives might use it. Your mother wouldn't take a penny for it though. Said she was glad it was in good hands.'

Ellie watched him chuckle, his blue eyes twinkling.

'Did you know my grandfather then?'

'Aye, we both lived here all our lives, went to school together. Was there when he married Beth, saw young Jim grow up.'

'My father,' whispered Ellie.

'When Beth died your grandfather wanted Jim to take up an apprenticeship, but he wasn't having any of it. He headed to London for a few years then came back to Dublin.'

'Where he met my mother?'

'Aye, your grandfather was pleased he was back in Ireland and that he'd settled down. They were very different people though. Your father was a genius of the mind, your grandfather a genius of the hands. That wooden bench outside was carved by your grandfather.'

'I saw it coming in.' Ellie headed out to take a closer look.

Jack followed the young girl and looked at her as she bent down beside the bench, running her hands over the wooden structure.

'There's amazing detail here,' said Ellie eyeing the curves and twists.

'A masterpiece all right. Your mother tells me you have your own pottery studio. I'd say the genius of the hands and mind lives on.'

A small smile formed itself on Ellie's face as she sat down on the wooden bench.

'It's good to see this,' and she tenderly stroked the wood beneath her fingers.

'You must have enjoyed going through the boxes.'

'What boxes?'

'In the back room, the photos and personal items were boxed for safekeeping.'

'I didn't go past the kitchen and living area.' Ellie rose.

Jack opened the bedroom door, they walked in and passed a bed covered by a white candlewick bed spread. Ellie watched him open an internal door and they stepped into a small room. A narrow bed stood by the wall, laden with cardboard boxes. She noticed a wooden box resting on a tall chest of drawers, knew it was carved by her grandfather. Opened it, to see an assortment of thimbles and threads.

'Do you want me to carry the boxes out to the living room for you?' asked Jack as he removed the yellowing newspapers that lay on top.

'No, no not at all, I'll be fine here.'

'Ruffles and I'll go and get some milk, there's tea and coffee in the presses. On a wet day we might leave our walk, light a fire and rest here a while,' but he knew he had lost her, lost her to the room and the history that lay within it. He watched her sit down on the side of the bed, open the boxes, and lift framed photos out. He retraced his steps, shook his head, a new sadness settling in his chest.

Ellie let her eyes rest on the black and white framed photo in her hand. Dark eyes looked back at her, a solid jaw line displayed by the tilt of the face. She moved from photo to photo, a multitude of people unknown to her. Then she recognised her father's photo. A similar one held pride of place in her mother's sitting room. She ran her fingers over the glass and then, saw it. That familiar feature of the jaw bone, a strength of character handed down from generation to generation. She placed her hand to her face and wondered.

Ellie went through box after box, eased out aged books and flicked through them. Clippings from newspapers and magazines, recipes and patterns folded within. She unveiled starched tablecloths and candlestick holders, gently replacing the items that she uncovered. Under an array of souvenir teacloths she found an assortment of mugs. Pulled them out and read the various place names: London, Germany and Galway. A deep desire filled her wanting to know more. Had these treasured items been presents or were they gathered memories each holding their own story? She looked around the small room, the boxes that she had sifted through, the lives that she had dipped into.

Ellie lifted the box of mugs and headed to the kitchen. She took down the plain white china cups and placed the mugs on the dresser. Sat at the table and spread her hands on her gently swelling stomach, felt the quiver of movement.

'You approve,' she whispered and felt a deep sense of love and peace settle within her.

The Quiet Whisper

Silence is stillness. Thoughts meander and calmness descends giving space and freedom. It's closing myself down to the outside world as I listen to the quiet whisper within.

Silence is the banging of a door in the distance, the rattle of a tea cup, the sigh as a realisation runs deep.

Silence is the hand that slips across the page.

Settling for Less

When we can no longer see the gems we are, as the chatter dims out the voice within. Standing forlorn hushed into submission. Our dreams cast aside, settling for less, no longer being true to ourselves.

As we pursue a path of cobbled stones, fearful of treading on possibility. We stumble into unknown territory reaching to grasp our truths.

Pat Griffin

I still have not received the Pulitzer Prize! After years of trying to figure out the secrets of successful writing I think I have found the answer. Twenty six! Letters in the alphabet, that is. They were used (with modest success) by Dickens, Shakespeare and Stephen King. All I have to do is get those same letters in the right combinations and I've got a sure fire bestseller! I'm working on the same system for the National Lottery numbers. If I can crack that I can live without the Pulitzer Prize! On a serious note, I have written and broadcast 'Thought for the Day' for radio and written comedy scripts for local theatre.

11

Platform 17 – Grand Central Station

by Pat Griffin

At 3.15 pm on the last Friday in April, Jenny Pickering Millet, 54 years old and unattached (she dislikes being called a spinster), stands up from her desk at the East 42nd Street Public Library.

'I have a train to catch, the 3.45 from Grand Central Station', she announces – for the second time that day. At 9 am that morning she arrived with a valise and a trace of a smile and said,

'I will be leaving a little earlier than usual today. I have a train to catch'.

On the last Friday in May, Jenny tidies her desk and prepares to leave her office, declaring that if she doesn't leave early she will miss her train.

'It is the 3.45 from Grand Central', she proclaims to her colleagues and then, after a momentary silence adds, 'Just like last month'.

She leaves the office carrying a valise, two bottles of wine and a neatly wrapped box emblazoned with the label *Leather & Lace*. At coffee break she had said, to no one in particular,

'Train to catch, must leave early today'.

Let us follow Jenny from the moment she arrives at Grand Central. She purchases her ticket and enters a carriage at Platform 17 East Lower Level. She does not settle herself too comfortably for she will depart the train two stops later. On leaving her carriage she walks two blocks to the Brookland Motel where she has booked a double room.

'I hope there is nobody here who knows me', she thinks, 'It would be so embarrassing. How would I ever explain myself?'

The receptionist recognises Jenny and says in a voice too cheery and too loud for comfort, 'Good to see you again. Either you're early or your guest is late. Doesn't really matter. Your room is ready. Just as you requested. Same as last month.'

Jenny would like to have said 'Shut your mouth, kid' But that type of language may be suitable in the movies, she thinks, but is not in Jenny's vocabulary. Instead she glances around the foyer to ensure that no one may have heard and replies in a whisper, 'Thank you.'

The receptionist hands her a room key. Jenny takes the elevator to the second floor and tries to ignore the musty smell which lingers on the corridor. She enters her room, but before she closes the door she makes sure to place the *Do Not Disturb* sign on the outside. She smiles to herself. She places her valise on the bed and blushes as she sees a hint of sheer black silk peeping from the edge of the case.

'Oh dear', she thinks, 'I hope nobody noticed.'

She opens the valise and removes the tissue wrapped package. She folds back the tissue paper to reveal a black negligee which she has bought by mail order.

'I could never walk into a store and buy one', she thinks. 'What would they imagine?'

She turns out each fold of the black negligee and lays it across the bed. She brushes her hands across the sheer black material and tries to smooth out the creases. A little more attention is needed to straighten the shoulder straps. She moves them an inch here and an inch there until they settle into just the correct position and thinks,

'Why, they are nothing more than threads. How easily they might snap – and what then?'

She steps back to see how it looks, spread out and wrinkle free, against the snow white bed spread. It looks almost perfect except for a small irregular fold which she notices across the bustline. She teases out the crease, brushes it smooth and feels a sudden rush of heat to her face. She checks her watch and looks again to be certain she has read the time correctly. The silent phone on the bureau attracts her attention. It might ring at any moment now, she thinks. From a cabinet she removes two wine glasses, opens a bottle of wine and fills both glasses.

Her handbag lies across the bed, almost snuggling up to the negligee.

She reaches into the bag and takes out a letter. Its contents she knows by heart but she reads it again and checks the time on her watch.

Jenny's arrival at the East 42nd Street Public Library at 9 am on the last Friday in June is announced by the clinking of wine bottles as she struggles through the revolving doors, dropping her valise and muttering 'Oh dear!'

Jenny does not allow herself the luxury of an angry expletive. Not even a good biblical 'Damn' passes her lips.

Jed Perkins, assistant chief librarian, rushes to help Jenny, picks up her valise and carries it to her desk. He notices that something black, soft and silky peeps from the edge of the valise. He makes no comment for he knows that to do so would embarrass Jenny. And yet he is just a little bit curious.

At 3.15 pm Jenny has left the library and rumours are rampant.

As the last week in July approaches, wagers are made and bets are placed by her colleagues at the East 42nd Street Public Library as to whether this month would see the continuation of the pattern which is so clearly emerging. Her early departure on the last Friday of each of the preceding three months confirms in their minds that 'Jenny is up to something!'

Of one thing they had always been certain – Jenny was predictable. At 54 years of age Jenny lived alone with two Persian cats, a parakeet and the '*Essential Recordings: The Great American Songbook*' on black vinyl (only analogue sound was acceptable to her ears). Jenny lived life to a pattern which only death could alter. Or so it seemed, until now.

On the last Friday in August Jenny leaves her desk at precisely 3.15 pm. She is followed by Jed Perkins who keeps himself at a safe distance from her as she approaches the ticket booth at Grand Central.

Just as discreetly he buys a ticket and follows her onto the train, ensuring that she does not see him. He is surprised when she gets off the train after two stops. On the following Monday morning Jed reports that Jenny arrived at the Brookland Motel.

'Beyond that', he adds, 'your guess is as good as mine!'

On the first Monday in September Jed Perkins arrives at the library. He is surprised to see that Jenny is not yet at her desk. There is an interruption during the coffee break when a courier enters the foyer of the

East 42nd Street Public Library.

'Delivery for Miss Pickering', he announces. He carries a floral bouquet. Jed Perkins accepts the delivery and places the flowers on Jenny's desk. Attached to the bouquet is a note. At coffee break Jenny has still not arrived.

Jed Perkins nods his head in the direction of Jenny's desk.

'She sure must be having one hell of a weekend, if you know what I mean,' declares Jed to his colleagues. He finishes with a wink as if to say 'Of course you all know what I mean'.

Curiosity has finally seized Jed Perkins with a grip which will not be denied. The note dangling from the bouquet of flowers just demands to be read, he reasons. Since Jenny is not here it seems a shame not to take care of her flowers. So, would it be such a crime if I accidentally happened to read the card, he thinks. He glances at the card. He is surprised to see the delicately embossed words *Discreet Dating*. He is even more surprised at his own insatiable curiosity as he sneaks a look at the rest of the message. *Thank you for your custom*, it reads. *Please accept this gift from us as a thank you for your continued custom. On your advice we will place your ad in our brochure. Just like last month. Our discretion is your guarantee.*

'I'll be damned', Jed whispers. 'The sly old dear. Who would have guessed'.

On the last Friday in September it is obvious that something has changed. Jenny arrives at her desk but on this occasion she does not carry a valise. Nor is her arrival heralded by the clinking of wine bottles or the rustle of delicately wrapped packages. Jenny moves a little slower and does not mention that she is leaving early. She avoids conversation. At coffee break she stays at her desk and appears nervous when her phone rings. She listens to hear what the caller has to say. She remains silent and hangs up the phone.

At 3.15 pm she stands away from her desk and looks to see that everything is in its proper place.

'I have a train to meet', she says.

She leaves her desk and shuffles through the revolving door and seems unaware of the teeming masses on East 42nd Street.

At Grand Central she purchases her ticket and moves to the escalator which takes her to the East Lower Level. She changes her mind and moves towards the stairs which will still bring her to Platform 17.

'Perhaps I will be quicker if I take the stairs', she reasons.

She checks her watch. It is 3.40 pm.

'Only another few minutes', she mutters.

She moves as quickly as she can down the crowded steps.

'Why are there so many people? It is never this busy,' she thinks. She stumbles and someone shouts, 'Hey, watch it lady, what's your goddamn hurry? Rushing for a fire or something?'

She does not seem to notice.

Another glance at her watch tells her that only a minute has passed since she last checked the time.

'Why is everything moving so slowly', she screams silently. 'I should have taken the escalator. '

She reaches the East Lower Level and pushes her way through the heaving bodies and finally reaches Platform 17. It is 3.42 pm. She checks the overhead monitor. Her train, she reads, will arrive at 3.45 pm. For the first time she seems to relax. Her shoulders sag. She sighs.

'I am on time', she says.

She walks across the platform. Someone seems to be shouting.

'So much noise', she thinks. 'So much noise.'

She sees someone wave at her.

'No, it cannot be me. He must be calling someone else', she thinks.

He is still waving, but everything seems to be moving as if in a dream, like wading through treacle. If she could only separate the sounds she might hear a voice scream at her,

'You're moving too close. Get back. Get back.'

But it is now 3.45 pm and she hears the rumble of the tracks as the train hurtles towards her.

'It is on time', she sighs. 'Always on time.'

Wax and Wood, Sailing Boats and Silent Skies

He leaned upon the garden wall and stared
and saw me play on vast expanse of grass
that was all exotic places to our childish minds – and he waved.

With those hands that could wave and weave and wax
he made shoes that bore the trademark of his skill.

He leaned across a homemade bench
and fashioned seasoned wood and dowel rods
into cricket bat, wicket and bails.
Those same hands could make boats with sails
and down at Kenny's Well we set them free.

He leaned across the kitchen table
and I watched as he was able
with ball of twine, brown paper and some sticks to make a kite.
We went to Daly's Hill and set it free to reach the silent sky.
He reeled out yards of twine and we watched it climb and climb.
'Cut the cord and set it loose,' I cried.

With those same hands that worked with strong grained wood
he'd gently tease a mushroom from the ground
or pick berries from a bush.
'We'll have fresh jam for tea tomorrow,' he'd say.

But late, much later still,
when time had played her tricks and stilled his hands
I leaned across the bed his nurse had made.
The father was a child and this son became a man
and my hands now nursed the man
who worked with leather and with wood.

Late, much later still,
I leaned across a box that other hands had made
and in that silent wooden frame my father lay,
hands clasping beads of wood and string.
'Cut the cord and set it loose,' I cried.

Back Then

The ice-cream van is back again.
Do you remember listening for the jingle jangle bell –
its promises of cold white ice on summer days?
Then you were small,
and wonder was as real as ice-cream,
dripping on your Sunday dress.
Grow small and let me clean that mess once more.

Mary Healy

Writing is like a treasure chest: it sparkles and glimmers from depths I have forgotten or may never have known.

My childhood was a series of summers swinging on a hammock under a sun dappled apple tree, days spent for the most part with my imagination and in the generous safety net of my father's glorious fields and my mother's harried preoccupation.

The third of five children, I was invisible and saw all and heard more than I should have.

I live in Kilkenny with my husband James and four children, a series of dogs and geriatric horses in one of the most beautiful places on earth.

I am grateful to be selected among the prize winners and honourably mentioned in the following competitions:

Fish Short Story 2011

Over the Edge Writer of the Year 2010

Penguin Eason/RTE Guide Competition 2010

Limerick Writers Centre December 2010

Creative Writing Inc 2010

Flash 500 Fiction 2010

12

Ancestors' Advice

by Mary Healy

She knew when they were coming; she could feel them first as vibrations, coming from where the sun rose. Gradually sound filled the air, waves of dust covering everything. Then the white strangers landed, like birds of prey and she waited yet again, for it all to begin.

They had been coming for many seasons now and she felt herself tense when the first sounds met her ears. She saw shadows fall on the other women's faces, watched their eyes change.

There was no hiding, here in the wide open plain where everything dried to colour that had no memory. They stood out with their black skin. The only landmarks on this horizon were the bleak trees. Even they dropped their leaves in defeat when the heat became too fierce. The cracks in the clay offered the only escape.

They tried to move away. The older people protested.

'This is where we have always lived. This is where our people are buried. Their spirits are near, we belong here.'

Maya could understand this. For them the next journey was the one that mattered.

For her, the present unbearable. Others said they were near water, how far would they have to go before finding a reliable source? They talked about it, and one time, even went to find a new place. Days of trudging, days of wandering in unfamiliar territory, facing new dangers, then waking to find themselves surrounded by people with menace on their faces. Her people had not been welcome.

They gathered up quickly and bundled themselves into the morning cold, afraid to look back.

After that there had been no question of going anywhere. They all knew that. So they stayed and waited. And when it was over; there was a sense of relief that it would be a while before they landed again. But for that day, the day they flew away, the place was wounded, the women were quiet, and you imagined they were weeping but there were no tears. The men were dark and hidden in their eyes, the light hurt them but there was something else, something other than the pain of too much drink.

She remembered the first night they took her. It was the summer she had grown tall, her legs like a gazelle's.

'You're so like Elsa,' her mother said, the shadow of pain darkening her face.

Elsa had been tall and graceful, proud and beautiful. The white men had said they would take her to see the city, where she could get work and have fine things. Maya remembered Elsa's face when she was leaving; her eyes bright and full of hope. Then the dust swallowed her.

They had set up camp and passed around food, offering drink to the men. As the night rolled on, their faces changed and Maya had seen the hunger in their eyes, the keen look of an animal on the prowl. She had always been told to steal away into the safety of the darkness. She heard the fear and warning in the women's voices. And she went quickly, without looking back. Madness had filled the air. She remembered the older ones taking the stranger's liquor, and drinking it fast, too fast for pleasure, too fast for anything but forgetfulness.

That night the campfire had burnt bright with wild flames. The men had eaten. She had a place where she went, but it was not safe there either. Wild animals hung on the edge of the darkness. Near the campfire, the threat had been no smaller.

She had moved away, melting into the shadow. A footfall behind had startled her. She turned and saw him there, the large white one, with the golden tooth and eyes the colour of sky. For a moment he had watched her, then smiled, slowly crooked his finger and extended his arm, a thick arm woven with muscle and pale coloured hair. And she had felt terror spike her sharply. As she sprang away she had stumbled, the ground dusty and firm beneath her fleeing feet.

She had made distance between them, she knew the scrubby thicket she was heading for and if she could get there… instead another shape had loomed out of the dark and caught her fleeing body, throwing her up in the air with ease. It was the other one, the one with the bandana and writing on his skin. He had held her, squirming and writhing, laughing into her face.

'My, a wild cat,' he leered.

Lying there she had remembered seeing a gazelle devoured by lions, the look in the animal's eyes, of bleak dread, when it was silenced by pain. Before it died the crunch of fine bone, and tearing of flesh, young blood leaking away into the dust. In that moment she had known that terror herself.

When they had finished, they stood over her in silence. She had felt herself torn and bloodied, grazed where the earth had ground her flesh. One of them had caught the rag of her dress, and thrown it toward her, the tail of it licking her leg. She had flinched, rolled into a small shape and lay there, the night claiming her skin.

When her mother had come to find her, Maya saw the bleak look on her face, the same expression she had wondered about before and Maya had understood. Now she knew.

And so it went on and in time she learned to drink like the other women, so that it didn't hurt so much anymore when their big muscled bodies bore down on her light bones.

Finally the time came when she could bear it no longer.

She remembered the elders and how they went into themselves in times of trouble. She began her fast and slowly the world receded and she journeyed inwards, falling back into the place she had come from, to where her ancestors now lived.

Day blended into night and she was surrounded by dark and silence. She arrived in a place that was timeless. There she stayed until they came to her, the elders and the ones who had journeyed on. The ones she had not seen for a long time. They were different now, happy and strong. All their ailments and diseases, all their pain and age fallen away, and they sat and spoke to her.

When they finished she knew what she had to do.

She walked into the plain, all day, even in the heat, to gather twigs from the yellow bark tree, a twisted, low tree that was rare and strange. She collected the pupae of small green beetles, some grasses that grew in the distance, bitter sharp plants that no animal touched. Maya made this journey collecting, harvesting, into a small pouch of fine fabric, then she began the long trek back, in silence.

The spell already begun.

And so they arrived and Maya saw the men watching the young

children and she knew the time had come. That evening the wind grew high and wild, she threw a handful of the bark on the fire. The men were sitting down wind, watching the dancing, they cheered and laughed, their voices raucous and hard, the flames burning between them and the dancers. Soon the bark began to work, the men felt sleepy and stupid. The women filled the men's drinks and kept smiling, throwing their own cups to the dark. After a while the men fell silent, asleep.

They bloodied the men with the blood of a kid goat, left the carcass of fresh flesh hanging in the breeze, doused the fire leaving them to the darkness.

During the night the place was filled with the sounds of the wild. The sounds of splintering bone, of flesh being torn, the sound of teeth on skulls. And in the morning the dust had covered almost everything.

A Christmas Delivery

by Mary Healy

He said he'd be back for Christmas. She believed him, he always kept his promises.

'I have to go, there's nothing here for me now, and it's only for six months.'

'I know,' she said, she knew he hated being out of work.

She didn't tell him about the baby until he had arrived.

'Why didn't you tell me? I wouldn't have gone.'

'I know,' she smiled through the tears.

The baby was due at Christmas time. A Christmas delivery.

She thought about him often, out there with the skyscrapers and bright city lights. She knew he was lonely, even though he did his best to disguise it.

'You're like the Empire State Building,' he'd laughed proudly as he studied her bump on Skype. She smiled back into his beautiful brown eyes.

She saw them coming to the door the night they came to tell her. She already knew from their faces before they opened their mouths.

'I know,' she whispered. The details didn't matter, he was gone.

Christmas Eve came and the baby was on its way. The nurses were extra nice, they knew the story, knew Tom. She heard their sharp intake of breath when they saw the newborn's face.

They handed the baby to her. A son, strong lively and perfect.

'My God, he's the image of Tom.'

As she looked in the baby's brown eyes she smiled.

'I know,' she said.

'He said he'd be back.'

Between the Tick and the Tock

What is silence? you ask. It is a promise, anticipation,
expectation.
It is the instant before we begin.
It is bated breath.
It is still.
It is the words of a lover, not yet spoken.
It is the space between seconds. Between the tick and the tock,
That is silence
Before the ask and answer, between the kiss and tell.

It is where hope still lives,
Silence is never, forever.

Sometime Liars

There is nothing original about sin
We all do it.
Sometime
The sanctimonious among us are just the best liars.

Orla Hennessy

Born in Co. Meath, having spent some time in Dublin, England, Belgium and France, I've finally settled in Co. Kilkenny with my husband, sons, and a feline muse called Jinks. For years, when not working, I dabbled in craftwork and painting. Writing was waiting in the wings.

13

The Back Nine

by Orla Hennessy

She was beside him putting on her makeup while he shaved. As she reached for her lipstick, he heard her asking, 'which one?' Bill was tempted to answer, but knew if he spoke out loud she would go again. She went anyway. He sighed and rinsed his razor.

Downstairs in the hallway, he passed the row of boxes on the floor with his handwriting on the sides claiming clothes, music, and mementos. He picked up his glasses from the empty sideboard in the living room. Their house was becoming a skeleton. Its soul was packed away and its heart was gone.

As he ate his breakfast, she was there again reading the newspaper, and not noticing the corner of it dipping in the butter. He tried to hold on to her image, but she went as quickly as she came. Not for the first time he noticed that it was only at home he could see her so clearly.

Tidying up, he concentrated on the day ahead, and soon found himself humming. He was looking forward to playing the championship golf course. He had been on its waiting list, and now Ian, his son in law had arranged his membership as a retirement present. The game today with Ian was to be his first as a member.

He put on a jacket and went out to his car. The photos he was bringing to his daughter Lana, were on the seat. He opened the packet and looked at them again. They were taken in the zoo the previous week. Giraffes and zebras in the background and his grandchildren squinting in the sun. He loved the one of Lana holding Minnie in her arms. Both of them looked so like her: fair hair, blue eyes, and round faces. She would still be alive as long as he could see them. Putting them back he decided to get a copy of that one for himself.

The trees on the road to the course were covered in a haze of fresh green buds. Houses looked ready to face the summer. Spring fever had painted walls and cleared weeds from pathways. Shrubs were blooming and lawnmowers hummed. He knew he had let his house and garden run down recently, but what did it matter? He had decided he wouldn't waste any more time doing things he didn't want to do.

The sun came out and a harmless breeze ruffled the trees around the golf club gates. When he reached the car park Ian was already there taking his clubs out. He pulled in beside him.

'Hello Bill. A great day,' Ian called. He was a tall man with brown curly hair and grey eyes.

'Perfect. And it feels great to be a member.'

'Yeah. You'll like it here. They're a friendly bunch. You'll be one of the lads in no time.'

They pulled their trolleys on to the first tee. Bill loved the broad green fairways bordered by mature trees, the immaculate greens, and even the clean cut bunkers. As he addressed the ball he was aware that he was enjoying every moment. It was always that way on a golf course. He was able to switch his mind off everything else and concentrate on the game. When he swung the driver, it connected perfectly. Thunk. The ball went straight down the fairway.

'Good shot,' Ian said, standing with one hand on his driver and the other on his hip. Perfectly dressed, he looked like an advertisement in a golf magazine.

'A good first drive anyway,' Bill said modestly. He was a natural player and had a low handicap. More than that, he always found that if he applied the advised mental approach to the game, to his own life, that he succeeded there too. All he had to do was imagine what he wanted, relax, act, and it happened. Most of the time.

They played the first nine, and, as there was no one behind them, took a break at the drinks stand by the tenth.

'You know Lana can't wait for you to move in. She'll love having you around, we all will.'

'Thanks, Ian. I'm looking forward to it myself.'

'All the packing done?'

'Most of it.'

They stood quietly for a while watching tiny figures in the distance moving around the course.

'Lana still misses her.' Ian said.

'Yeah. They were very close.'

'How are you doing now? Since you gave up work?'

'Fine. I was afraid I'd miss it. But I don't. Not one bit. It's great to have time for this.'

After an enjoyable back nine, they drove the short distance to his daughter's house for lunch. As he pulled into the driveway he saw two little faces looking out of the living room window. Then they disappeared. He knew they had been standing on the couch watching out for him. When their mother opened the door they rushed out, took hold of his hands and pulled him in. Lana was wearing a simple yellow dress reflected in the bunch of daffodils on the hall table. She hugged him, and they went through to the kitchen.

'How did it go?' she asked.

'I took five euros off him,' Bill replied.

She gave Ian a sympathetic smile. Minnie and Jack were dancing around with excitement. The little girl whispered to her mother:

'Can I Mam? Can I?'

'Yes.'

They ran away and came back carrying parcels. Minnie handed him hers with one arm outstretched, and the other behind her back.

'Happy Birthday, Granddad.'

She waited three seconds and then tore at the wrapping. It was a brown teddy bear. Bill looked at Lana, who looked back apologetically.

'She insisted.'

'He's for your room. You have no teddy,' Minnie said.

They laughed, and Minnie turned her chin towards her shoulder.

'Thanks Minnie. He's lovely,' he said hugging her.

'Has he a name?'

'No. You have to name him.'

'I'll call him Toto, then.'

'Follow the yellow brick road,' his daughter hummed.

Jack's present was a painting he had done of his family. Lana and Ian, himself and Minnie, and his Granddad in a blue shirt with short spiky hair. She wasn't in it.

'You can put it in your room. If you want.'

Bill cleared his throat.

'I certainly will. Thanks Jack.'

'Will we put it up now?'

'Yeah. OK.'

'And Toto too,' said Minnie.

'And Toto too.'

He followed them up the stairs to his room. Lana and Ian had wanted to give him theirs but he wouldn't have it. This one was big enough and had a view of the street. He had yet to bring some of his furniture, but there was a wall of shelving for his books. They hung the picture, and Minnie tucked the teddy up in his bed.

Downstairs they dished out the roast lamb lunch and sat down. They chatted about little things. Minnie's argument with her friend over a game, a film Ian had watched the previous night, and how Bill had chipped a ball out of an awkward lie. For dessert Lana produced a birthday cake. The children knelt on their chairs to be near it. Both of them scooped their fingers in the cream on the side, sucked them and giggled. Lana opened a box of candles.

'How many is sixty-five?' Jack asked his Granddad.

'Too many,' Bill said laughing.

'Five will do,' said Lana.

'But I'm five.' Jack gave him a puzzled look.

They sang Happy Birthday and Minnie blew out the candles.

'Minnie, whose birthday is it?' asked Lana.

'Granddad's. Do it again.'

'Will you help me blow them out Jack?' Bill asked.

He did, and they all clapped.

After lunch Bill went with Lana and the children to the park nearby. He held Minnie's soft little hand as she skipped beside him. It could have been Lana's. He had loved every day of her life, and had found it hard to let her go at the altar. When they came in sight of the swings and slides, the children ran ahead to join the eager gang, unrestrained by adults; free in their own world. They ran from one brightly coloured fixture to the other as if wanting to try them all at the same time. Relaxed mothers and anxious grannies waited on benches. Lana and Bill sat with them.

'Remember my old swing in the back garden? How Mam wouldn't watch when you swung me higher and higher?'

'Yeah. I remember.'

He had completely forgotten. His life with her was like pieces of film. Some of it would never be looked at again.

'Dad. I wanted to ask you something. You know Jack's starting school in September.'

'Yeah.'

'And Minnie will be starting playschool at the same time. We were wondering, would you mind taking them to school? And maybe pick them up in the afternoon. It would mean we'd both be free to get to work earlier, and get home earlier.'

Bill didn't have to think about it. He was pleased she had asked.

'Yeah. I'd love to. No problem.'

'Are you sure? They can be a handful.'

'I don't mind. I can manage them.'

'Thanks Dad. You know we both love you minding them. In their lives. You know.'

'Yeah. I know.'

They were suddenly both sad, thinking how much she would have loved to look after them too. It was a sweet joy made bitter. With tears in his eyes he watched Minnie running from one swing to the other, and Jack testing himself on the ropeway.

Later that evening as they waved him off, loneliness crept inside him like a ghost.

When he arrived home, he stood for a while in the silent hall before going into the living room.

Their books were all packed. A library of memories. Read in the garden, beside the fire, in planes, on beaches. There was the one they both couldn't wait to read, so they agreed to take turns reading chapters.

'Aren't you done yet? You're cheating.'

'No I'm not.'

The only things left to pack were photos. They were all around the house. She was in every one, and he couldn't bring himself to put her face up in a box. He slumped on the couch, and stared for a long time at the keys in his hands. He was being pulled in both directions and was tired of it. He got up, poured a glass of whiskey and took a big gulp. Outside on the patio he sat in the pale light from the kitchen. The sun had gone down and it was getting cold. She was standing in front of him in her blue parka, pressing the studs closed. She smiled at him.

Some time later he was in the living room punching the bottoms out of empty boxes and folding them. All their books were back on the shelves.

Payne's Grey

by *Orla Hennessy*

I wake up early, still obsessed. I was dreaming about it again. Holding my arms up and outwards, sweat pouring from every pore in my body. Since I came home, it has grown at the back of my mind, colouring my days, and insisting that I put it on canvas. Today, I'm ready.

Coffee pot in hand I go down the path to my studio. The air is misty. It's a sign. I make room on the bench, take the half finished painting off the easel, and put up a fresh canvas. Placing my hand on its sterile surface, I know I will give it life. I find some clean brushes and knives, and scrape the palette clean. Finding the right colours - mostly blues and yellows to make the greens - I squeeze out their buttery contents.

Through the skylight I see the fog is still there, but I'm in the jungle, wading through damp foliage, trying to keep leaves out of my eyes. My boots slip on mossy roots as I try to keep pace with the others. The high canopy of trees blocks out the direct sunlight, and leaves me in a sea of heavy greens.

I tame the canvas with a wash of terre verte, and the sight of it sucks me in. Mixing paint quickly, I spread the mixture in broad strokes. Layers of branches and leaves grow into each other, and trailing vines hang down like giant string beans. One suddenly whips in front of my face, and then moves away as a spider monkey curls his tail around it and swings to the next tree.

I move the paint around with big brushes. All my senses are tuned in now. The noise around me is deafening. Chattering and whooping monkeys, screeching birds, and, in the background, the constant hum of insects. In places I scrape the tops of branches with a knife to let in light, and spread the leaves of rubber plants with viridian. The hot air is saturated with moisture and the smell of strange fruit and herbs. Suddenly, there is a small frog sitting on a branch, inches from my eyes. A perfect watery creature, emerald green with crimson eyes. His taut slippery skin pulses to his heartbeat.

Much later I leave them, and move up the canvas on my own. The colours become lighter and the taller trees more scarce. The path is steep and the jungle less intense. I hurry to beat the dark. It is getting foggy but the way is clearer. Paler greens and misty blues. Brush. Brush. Brush.

I have arrived on a higher plane and am standing in the open. The canopy forms rolling hills all the way to the horizon. The sun is gone, leaving a pale gold wash, dimming as the minutes pass. The full moon takes shape, sharper and sharper until I can see its craters. A Payne's Grey fog rises like steam from the trees to form a soft blanket. The blue sky deepens, and zinc white stars pierce the blackness over my head.

At last, it's done, and I'm free again.

I look up, and the same moon looks down on me.

Time Out

Silence is when we can ignore all the sounds around us. Then, new thoughts will come out to play.

Stella Lanigan

Growing up on the Tipp Kilkenny border my parents instilled in me a great sense of pride of place especially during the hurling season and to this day my passion for hurling and support for Tipperary is as strong as in my childhood. After completing a secretarial course I worked in Dublin for a few years before returning to my home parish where I now live with my husband and six children. We live on a dairy farm where I do little work but love to walk and keep in touch with nature. I work in the local community playgroup, like listening to music and play guitar badly. I joined the creative writing course in 2009 and it has been blamed for my poor housekeeping and given me the perfect excuse to avoid my husband and hide from my children when needs be.

14

Grandfather

by Stella Lanigan

The first time I ever saw a dead man was when my grandfather died. I was ten. He lived with my grandmother down a boreen just outside the village. Any free time I had I spent there; it gave me my first feelings of independence.

Even though he worked hard for many years as a farm labourer, my grandfather's appearance remained the same. On weekdays he wore old clothes. A tweed cap sat slightly to one side of his head. On Sundays he'd dress up in his only suit and tie and saved his top coat for very cold days. Proud of his reputation for punctuality amongst his family and friends he'd constantly check his pocket watch, reminding my grandmother to hurry or they'd be late for first Mass. When the lament would finally get to her she'd throw her eyes up to Heaven and say:

'Merciful hour, you'd think we had miles to go the way you go on.'

Then she'd gently place her rosary beads inside her coat pocket, and put her prayer book carefully into her handbag. Closing the door behind her, my grandmother would head for the black Hillman Hunter parked in the yard, knowing that not only would they be in plenty of time for Mass but she would probably end up doing the Stations of the Cross just to pass the time.

If you didn't know my grandfather you could easily have mistaken his occupation, such were his physical features and fine manners. He seldom stood still but when he did he was as tall as a tower. His shoulders stretched in a straight line across the top of his back giving a strong square shape to his upper body. His hands were huge and as rough as sandpaper. But what I loved most was his broad smile, it softened his whole appearance. He loved the company of others and never had a bad word to say about anyone. The cottage was a place of regular gatherings for card drives and music sessions. He often sang and played the mouth harp. His favourite song being 'Cod Liver Oil.' He liked his bottle of stout and smoked a solid oak Kapp and Peterson pipe, with a down turned stem and brass band. It was a present from the Maguires when he retired after a lifetime of tending to the horses on the estate.

I was always fascinated by the ritual of pipe smoking. It was my job to buy the half quarter of Yachtsman tobacco in Phelan's every Saturday morning, then cycle the few miles down the road knowing that a bag of liquorice sweets would be waiting for me. With his penknife, my grandfather would carefully slice off a portion of tobacco then, placing it in the palm of his hand, break it up into little pieces before packing it into his pipe like putty. The remainder went into his pouch. He'd strike up a match and light the tobacco, then putting his finger over the opening he'd begin to suck, allowing it to ignite. His jaws would sink inwards, then suddenly you'd hear the pop of the pipe on his lips. To amuse his grandchildren he would often make circular smoke come from the pipe which reminded us of the cowboys and Indians films we'd seen on television, when the Big Chief would smoke the peace pipe.

On the day of his funeral his grandchildren were made stand and look at him as he lay in the coffin. My mother explained to us that grandfather had gone to God. He was going to Heaven where Paddy Casey and Ned Ryan had gone the previous year. They had lived down in Leek and were good friends of his. Their dying didn't bother me but his did. Who'd pick the potatoes for my grandmother? Who'd save the turf in summer? Who'd look after the horses for Maguires when Michael was away? Would there be any more parties now that he was gone? I had a lot of questions to ask but no one to answer them. Everyone was too busy.

For three days a constant stream of people kept coming and going to the cottage. Each of them had the same thing to say.

''Tis well he's looking.'

Old Mrs. Walsh sighed as she stood at the side of the coffin. With a sprig of palm in her hand she sprinkled my grandfather with Holy Water from a small bowl left standing on a table.

'He really looks himself Mary,' said Katie Maguire as she shook my grandmother's hand.

'Sure does any of us know the day or the hour we're destined to leave this place? We must always be ready. We'll pray for his soul God Rest Him,' sighed old Mrs Walsh again while shaking her head and making the sign of the cross.

I disagreed quietly to myself as nobody else would listen. None of it made any sense to me. How could someone who was constantly doing things for himself and others 'be like himself'? As I looked at him lying inside the coffin all I saw was the stillness of his body with a waxy look on his face of faded yellow. His hands were clasped tightly around his rosary beads. I had never seen them so clean or felt them so cold. The only form of life inside his coffin now was a fly moving around his forehead. As I watched I wondered could my grandfather bring up his hand with force to make him go away as I had seen him do so many times before in the garden, cursing them while waving his cap in frustration.

Uncle Tom took charge of everything. He picked the coffin of elm, with heavy brass handles mounted on both sides top and bottom. A white lining ran along the inside which reminded me of my grandmother's satin slip worn only for special occasions. Otherwise it was placed with her precious possessions in a trunk in her bedroom, wrapped in a brown paper bag. The lid stood upright against the wall, the crucifix attached. Four shiny screws sat on each corner.

The breast plate showed the following:

James Ryan
Died
10th March, 1979
Age
71 years.

My grandmother was sitting on a chair by the window, tears in her eyes. Her daughters tended to her every need. Her sons greeted the relatives and friends. The women went straight over to my grandmother while the men gathered outside or in clusters about the house. My uncle's offerings of whiskey and stout were not refused. When the gravediggers arrived he shook each of them by the hand, while slapping them firmly on the shoulders saying.

'Thanks a million lads. 'Twas tough going down there, especially when ye hit rock.'

'Twas nothing,' came their replies as their feet shifted about the floor, uneasy with the compliments that were given. They listened and nodded attentively while my uncle continued to talk about the hole they'd dug in the ground.

'Six foot by three foot,' I heard them say.

Then finally they were released from his snare by the cries of an inebriated neighbour.

'Did you ever hear tell of a wake in Ireland that ran out of whiskey? It would be an awful shame if this be the first,' as he held up his empty glass, waiting for attention. My uncle beckoned to his two brothers who helped the man quietly from the room.

All the while my cousins played in the garden. Each time I went out to them my eyes were drawn to the turf that was stacked neatly to one side of the shed. Everywhere I looked I could see signs of the many summer months we'd spent together in the garden. The daffodils we'd planted were just beginning to bloom. The swing he'd made for me was hanging idle from the bare branch of the cherry blossom tree. The rope we'd bought in Phelan's, the tyre had come off an old trailer thrown on its back above in the farmyard.

'They won't even miss it,' he'd said with a wink as we walked back down the lane.

I played for hours on it the very first day, my grandmother shouting at me:

'Get down or you'll be sick from swinging.'

My grandfather laughed and said:

'Leave her be, she'll get tired of it soon enough.'

All these thoughts were in my head and it wasn't long before I'd find myself back inside standing beside the coffin. I was beginning to realise that things would never be the same.

As far as I was concerned my grandfather knew everything. No one could replace him. He was the one to decide when the time was right and, along with my father and Uncles Tom and Jimmy, they would head off down to the bog. My mother and I would arrive at lunch time laden down with baskets of sandwiches, flasks of tea with sugar and milk added, freshly made scones and currant cake.

The bog came alive in the summer. Most of the people in the parish had a plot. There was a great sense of community as everyone gathered to save the turf for winter. The surface of the bog was covered in light brown dust and with the slightest breeze it could be lifted up. If we weren't careful it would catch us in the eye causing a temporary blindness. If we could see it coming we'd bury our heads in our hands for protection. But when the digging began that was a different story, the turf became dark and dirty, sticking to our hands and settling in under our nails. My grandfather always insisted on being down in the pit with Uncle Tom. My father and Uncle Jimmy stayed on top to catch the turf as it flew from the sheaf and over my grandfather's shoulder. Once caught it would be passed on before being placed on top of the ground to dry. This process would go on well into the evening until the sun began to settle. Then everyone would walk home together, arranging a time for the next morning.

'A bright red sky at night is always a good indicator of a fine day to follow,' my father would say, checking out the weather conditions on the way home, and he was rarely proven wrong.

Fr. McGrath decided it would be best to bury my grandfather on Friday. But my Uncle Sean had not arrived home from England. My grandmother was beginning to get anxious. She was assured that he had received the news and would no doubt be on the next boat from Holyhead to Dun Laoghaire. Then he'd get the bus down from Dublin and Michael Maguire would kindly pick him up in his car. Late into the second day my uncles also began to worry as there was still no sign of Sean. They knew their mother wouldn't hear tell of a burial until the boy was home.

'I wouldn't be surprised if that scoundrel didn't bother to show up,' my father said to my mother in the kitchen.

'Don't be like that Pat,' she replied. 'It can't be easy facing back after all these years, knowing you have to bury your father into the bargain.'

'Well, 'twas his fault they left on bad terms,' came his reply. 'He'll get no sympathy here.'

'Can't you just let bygones be bygones for mother's sake?' she pleaded. 'I want no trouble these next few days.'

'You needn't worry about me, Brid,' he replied. 'But I can't answer for your three brothers.'

'Ah! Will you have a word with them, Pat, please for Heaven's sake?' sighed my mother.

'I will, I will,' he said. 'But I can't promise anything though.' Blessing himself he left the room.

Grateful for Silence

Silence is something I seldom get to appreciate; such is my life. But today I am given an opportunity to sit with it for a few moments and see where it takes me.

Surrounded by my friends, I sit in silence and hear the pressure of pens on paper as people are busy with their thoughts. A door squeaks and there is an echo throughout the hallway. Even though it's winter the humming of the heating system overhead reminds me of a swarm of bees in summer. Muffled voices penetrate the walls from a room next door. I hear a spoon clanking in a cup in the kitchen. The shuffling of someone's feet as they shift from side to side in their seat.

A gush of wind finds its way through the window behind my back. My senses are becoming more in tune with nature as it lifts the hair on my neck and sends a cool breeze around my back.

There is a peace at present, one that I seldom get to sit with in my day to day life. I am grateful for this time.

A Child's Riddle

As a child I was constantly reminded of what a sin was. It wasn't the big ones that I was afraid of, like a mortal sin, because they were for big people and really bad ones – I was a child. It was the little ones I feared the most. They ones my mother kept reminding me of. It was a sin to back answer your parents, for instance, or if you were caught laughing or talking in Mass, 'Well... may God forgive you', was what my Grandmother used to say.

But the person I feared even more than my parents was the priest when he visited our school. He would constantly remind us of our sinful ways and put the fear of God in us. I felt hard done by because a lot of the time I didn't know what he was talking about. Two boys who lived down the road from me smoked and were caught on numerous occasions mitching school but still by sixth class they didn't seem any different to me. They had not developed any physical features that would show they had sinned. 'It's not outside that you will notice these things', my Grandmother would preach, 'It's the soul them boys will have to worry about, when their time comes to crossing over.'

As we got older the big one was sins of the flesh. It was assumed that if you were in the company of the opposite sex that sins of the flesh were committed. You were doomed to Hell for all eternity at such a crime.

PJ McAuliffe

I've been described as one of life's resilient characters, a true survivor, with an impish sense of humour and a great laugh. This will do me; I'm from Finglas and live in Waterford city. I work for FÁS, that and writing are the two constants in my life. I love the Irish countryside and its people and I try to express this in my stories. I enjoy the company of family and friends and driving my Opel car.

15

Identical Twins

by PJ McAuliffe

Josephine Maher, from her earliest recollection wanted to be a Mercy nun. She now had that chance at eighteen years of age with a good Leaving Certificate in her hands. The vocations director for the Mercy order was glad of her; she was the only recruit in the Cork dioceses that year which was unusual in itself.

Josephine, a blue eyed, black haired, pretty girl of slim build had a major task ahead. She knew that the lads in her local village of Newmarket called her the hugger, the altar hugger that is. Josephine was a deeply religious girl, got it from her mother, she loved calling into the church to pray to God, she helped out too with religious ceremonies, adoration came easy to her and she had a special affection for the Blessed Virgin. She often lit a penny candle for both her deceased grandparents.

There was more good news from Kanturk a village just five miles north east where David her friend had just got his results. He too would be able to progress his vocation to be a priest in the Cork dioceses. In a year's time he would start his theological and philosophical studies in University College Cork. Josephine joined him at university after she completed her preparation years with the Order; she studied social science as she was interested in helping disadvantaged people.

It would be twelve years to her final vows, before that she had to complete her degree, work abroad most likely in Africa, and spend time in retreat. She would not be taking her final vows until she was thirty years of age.

Sister Josephine as she addressed herself was undaunted by the programme of work. She was not upset by the absence of people of her own age in the Mercy community, her vocation, her calling, was special to her as it was to her friend David.

It brought joy to her heart to meet David each day at college; they were a source of strength to each other and found it easy to discuss and share their religious faith. Their passage through college went smoothly; essays were in on time and exams passed. They passed their finals and both their parents were extremely proud of this achievement and their families shared in a celebratory meal in the Metropole Hotel in Cork city. Josephine felt that the rest of her journey towards final vows would be somewhat easier as it was mostly related to work that she had a deep interest in. She quit her comfortable digs on the Western Road and went to work as an outreach assistant in the hospice on Clyde Road. She spent her time consoling relatives of cancer patients who were in the final stages of life.

The religious pictures that hung from every wall in the hospice brought a sense of foreboding to anyone that walked its corridors. Josephine eased the panic of the relatives but the humdrum of the morphine pump even got to her and it became a recurring sound in her head for a time. Her religious observations such as morning prayer, daily Mass and vespers sustained her through this time but her experience of life's dance with death brought a slight troubling to her, a troubling she could not rightly identify.

Josephine was losing touch with her friend David, considered by their friends as twins when they were at school and college. He had been transferred to Dublin. They had talked about this troubling feeling she had, he never had anything like it and he assured her it would pass. David's ordination would take place in another year and they agreed to meet for that.

The transfer she was looking forward to, came through and she was off to Dublin. Now eight years into her vocation she found herself in Ballymun, doing the work she liked, helping the community. The Mercies had a small operation there two nuns and two associates working out of a small office. One great advantage was that she did not have to wear a nun's habit; she melted in better, but everyone knew she was a nun. And she played this card if she really wanted to get something done.

Josephine felt happy in the city, helping the poor and educating the ignorant, after all she was in the city of Sister Catherine McAuley the Mercy Order's founder. She stayed at night in their community house near Baggot Street.

'What a nice place this is,' Josephine muttered, 'and just beside the Grand Canal, it will be nice to walk there on Sunday mornings after Mass.'

True enough she would sit there on Sunday morning quietly observing the still water disturbed only by the gliding swans, two of them.

The tall flat complex of Ballymun turned grey when heavy rain fell, which was often. It was on one of those wet days, nine years into her training and three years from her final vows that Paddy came through her office door.

'It's me that decides who gets the flats around here,' said Paddy. The twenty-six-year-old housing officer with Dublin Corporation was in a rage and mad as hell.

'I've a homeless family standing outside on the road, all because a Josephine or whatever her name is, gave a vacant flat to someone else; this is a big problem for me at two o'clock in the afternoon Ballymun time. Those bloody do gooders are a real pain in the ass.'

Josephine could feel the rage.

'Calm down! Calm down,' she cried, 'and I'm Josephine. Who are you anyway?'

Paddy was standing there in his blue overcoat, wringing wet.

'I'm the man from Dublin City Council.'

But, Paddy felt a deep back pedalling going on inside him. He felt he was walking forward but going back the way. He had already worked out where to put the family who was now standing at the lift wall. Again he repeated, as if she did not hear him the first time. He wiped his wet hair with a bit of tissue she had given him. Again he repeated in a softer tone:

'I'm from the City Council...it's okay; I'll get somewhere else for the family to stay.'

Paddy had met a girl, and she was now inviting him into her office for a cup of tea which was the Mercy way. As Josephine handed the tea to Paddy he noticed the cup was in a saucer and there was a spoon on the saucer and a Marietta biscuit. As for Josephine, she tried to hide the attraction for Paddy...he looked just like David, and talked like him. But there was more, a type of protection in him. They became embarrassed as they looked at each other, just two twenty-six-year-olds in an office in a flat in Ballymun having a cup of tea.

'Would you have dinner with me?' He blurted out. Something he had never done before.

'Yes, I will.' Something she absolutely never did. But there you go, a man and a woman, as they say.

'You're what?' he said, raising his voice above the other diners.

'I'm sort of a student nun.' Josephine knew Paddy would not know the ins and outs of religious life and he sounded like a guy that did not have much religion himself anyway.

'Jesus,' he murmured to himself, he had hopes here, so she's a nun. But he looked at her face, thought of her stand, her eyes and talk, her sound...this was not going to be easy. But it was easy, she felt as he did.

You see Josephine had not taken her final vows, the hardest part would be telling her parents, her vocations director and David. Paddy made a decision that he would support Josephine no matter what happened. That decision was never displayed not even to Josephine, but it was something more that she noticed when she first met him.

She walked up the long timber floored hall to the desk of the vocations director and explained she was leaving because she had met Paddy. Her resignation was accepted in kindness and gratitude. Her parents too accepted with difficulty her decision but David was happy for her. 'It looks like the twins will have to separate out' was all he ever said.

This closed an important chapter in her life, now Josephine had to create a new life for Paddy and herself in Dublin city. They married, and settled into life on the northside of Dublin just like thousands of other young married couples. She found herself pregnant with twins – identical twins according to her doctor at the maternity hospital in Parnell Square. It was in the hospital that she again met up with David. Fr David was now the chaplain of the hospital. She had missed his ordination as he had been ordained in Rome.

As they talked of old times Josephine could see that David was very happy, he loved what he did. He liked being the centre of attention. He was still very thin, smart and well liked. He was rock solid in his faith.

The 3D scans showed the twins developing normally, at twenty weeks their heads, back bone and limbs were all beginning to join up.

Later it was discovered that because they were identical one twin was taking all the blood and the other twin was slowly being deprived of life. The weak twin would die if a corrective operation was not carried out. The procedure, delicate as they all are, required the incision of a miniature camera followed by a miniature laser, its purpose to burn off surplus blood vessels that had developed on the healthy twin and was taking all the blood.

Doctors explained to Paddy and Josephine that failing to carry out this procedure would result in the death of the weak twin and the procedure if carried out could result in the death of both. There was that risk.

They were in a kind of haze that separated them from reality. Josephine asked to see David, who rushed to the consulting rooms to console them.

'What are we going to do?'

But Fr David felt a bit confused too, and did not answer. He held tight to Josephine's hand.

She needed to get out of the hospital, just away, as if movement would get her away from the problem. As Paddy and Josephine walked along the corridor David decided to let them have their own space, but as they left he whispered to both to have the operation.

Paddy asked her where they should go.

'Ah Paddy just to get some air, just to sit in a place that was quiet, a place like Baggot Street, near the canal where I used to sit on Sunday mornings and watch the two swans,' said Josephine.

This is how Josephine and Paddy came to be sitting on a park bench in the Garden of Remembrance on a sunny day at the end of July. Paddy left her side just for a while to fetch her something cool to drink. As she watched him walk down by the pool, shaped in a cross, calmness descended on her. It could have been the church spire a block away that reminded her of the church spire in Newmarket, but the calmness helped her to see the bright colours of the flowers around her and the beautiful green grass. The clear water in the pool reflected back to her the clarity in which she saw things.

She saw Paddy and herself as identical twins, a balance between men and women, in the cross the twins of the finite and the infinite, in the hospice the twins of life and death and the imbalance that disturbed her there. As Paddy walked back towards her carrying two cardboard cups, she thought of the twinned life growing inside her and now she must save them both and risk losing both. As they sat there on the park bench they settled on having the procedure.

On their way back to the hospital she recalled that the troubling feeling she'd had in the hospice never recurred after she met Paddy. She held his hand gently and then he muttered:

'It's funny how a Garden of Remembrance Memorial ends up beside a maternity hospital.'

The Universe in the Silence

I'm one of the lucky ones; I know it's there, the silence. Aside from the heartbeat in my ear, it is there, a resonance with a sound I need silence to hear, the sound of the universe.

There is a difference between silence and sound. Silence is not the absence of sound, but we need to be silent to hear the sound. Om, Om, that is what it sounds like, you will hear it if you are silent long enough, then you will know.

Its beat is rattling on all the time, if it were not, we would not be here.

Rachel Nolan

When I was ten I asked my mother why I was so much smaller than the other children in my class. She told me not to worry, that I would make my mark on the world even if I had to use tiny feet to do it.

My first writing step came with the publication of my first story at eleven. I wish I had savoured that moment because it would be a long time before I saw it again.

Life has taken me down many different paths but I've always travelled them with wonderful people, with courage and always in my fabulous shoes.

16

Her Green Boots

by Rachel Nolan

Mark watched from the shadows as John's hand lingered on Katie's bare knee. She swept back her hair in a gentle teasing motion, with the arch of her eyebrow he knew. The sick feeling in his stomach rose to find its home in his throat. He knew but simply refused to accept it. Fear of loneliness is a dangerous thing. But his eyes could not renounce what his heart already felt.

He slipped silently out of the hotel lobby; no confrontation tonight. He tried to erase the picture from his mind; after all, he still loved her. But he couldn't see any way out of this. Moving through the dark streets he didn't know where to go. He couldn't bear the thoughts of going back to their house. It was bathed in the scent of Katie, she was everywhere in the home they had built together. Every inch of it assembled with love and affection. He walked back to his car, sat inside and fought the tears.

Katie sipped on the glass of chilled Chardonnay as John's hand slowly traced the softness of her inner thigh. Her guilt quickly replaced by the greedy pangs of desire. Putting the glass down on the table she leaned in close to him. Lying to Mark didn't suit her, but she couldn't help herself. She could feel the threat of an engagement looming and she wanted to be sure that if she married Mark it was out of love and not loyalty. She smiled as John beckoned for the bill and all other thoughts conveniently escaped her memory.

John paid the bill and led her up the stairs. He loved the cliché of meeting in the hotel lobby for drinks, it added to the excitement. Once Katie had two glasses of wine she would always feel a little less guilty. They had met a few times in his house, but truthfully his house just wasn't exciting enough. As he watched her shapely body walk up the stairs he knew he was already growing tired of her.

Mark's phone rang. He let it ring out. The hollow tone resonated and he tried to allow nothing but that to occupy him. He still wasn't sure where to go. He couldn't stay here for the duration of the night; the coldness was starting to creep in through the cracks in the car door and the tears on his shirt collar only added to the chill on his neck. He started the engine but still wasn't sure if he could face going home. From the moment he had introduced him, he had seen the spark. Katie always reassured him, saying:

'John is the type of guy who buys you drinks all night and the morning after pill the next day, you're the kind of guy to kiss you goodnight and buy you dinner the next evening'.

In a way this always bothered Mark. He remembered the note he had seen on the fridge that morning and he started to cry again.

I'll be late tonight but meet you in bed about 10.

K

Xxxx

P.S. have you seen my green boots?

John was aware of the effect he had on women. He always admired Katie, but that all changed once he finally seduced her. Now the thrill of sleeping with her was swiftly being replaced by a monotonous pattern of unoriginal meetings. He sat on the end of the bed and watched her as she slipped back in to her dress. This was the last time he wanted to see her.

Katie could feel his eyes on her. She turned around and caught the look on his face. It was one of triumph and it made her feel disgusting, shameful and guilty. She picked up her handbag from the dresser and left without a word. The game was over and she knew she had lost.

She had no great plans to tell Mark and she knew John would never tell him either. She sat in her car trying to convince herself that she would simply put this behind her and never think about it again. She caught her reflection in the rear view mirror and started to cry.

Mark pulled up at the house and was surprised to see Katie's car outside. He watched her through the window for a few minutes. Her long dark hair moved gently, caught by the breeze from the open window.

The soft light from the lamp touched her skin and when she turned she looked beautiful.

Katie heard Mark's car in the drive. She checked herself in the mirror one last time to see if she had washed all the guilt off her face. It took him a little longer than usual to come in but she was thankful for it. She heard the key in the lock and a sense of fear and panic gripped her. What if she never heard Mark's key in the door again?

When he came into the kitchen she walked over and kissed him.

'Why are you so late hunnie?'

'You were the one who left a note saying you were going to be late.'

'Oh yeah, I got out of work early and I told them that I'm sick of doing all these late nights, so I don't think I have to do them any more. Isn't that great? I get to spend more time with you.'

He didn't respond and Katie knew she was talking too much and too fast. She wanted something, anything, to puncture the heavy silence she was afraid would reveal her shame. Words were failing her so she kissed him again, but harder. She caught his hand and led him to the bedroom. He started undressing her but then he stopped. He looked at her and walked away. The front door slammed and she ran to the window calling him, but if he heard he didn't respond.

Mark saw her eyes when she kissed him. She was sorry and he knew it. As he undressed her, he tried hard not to imagine John's hands touching her and John's lips on her breast, but he couldn't. He needed to know if she was back because she wanted him or because she ran out of options. He gently pushed her away from him and walked out of the house. He heard Katie calling him.

John was at home enjoying a beer when he heard the car pull up. He recognised the rumble of the engine as Mark's. He swallowed the rest of his beer in one go and waited impatiently for the doorbell to ring. It didn't. Opening the door he was met by a swift punch. He staggered back with a heavy thud and fell to the ground.

'Jesus Christ man, what the fuck?'

Mark said nothing; he just picked up a pair of green boots next to the rubbish bin by the door. Before John could say another word Mark hit him again and left.

'Hey love, are you okay? What was that about earlier? Where did you go, I was really worried?'

'I went for a drive.'

'You felt like going for a drive just as we were about to –?'

Before she could finish he walked over and kissed her hard.

'What's got into you today?' Katie giggled.

Later on that night as Katie lay in Mark's arms, she could feel his slow breathing on her neck but she knew that he wasn't asleep.

'Mark?'

'Yes.'

'I love you.'

'I love you too.'

'Mark?'

'Yes.'

'Have you seen my green boots anywhere?'

'No love, I haven't seen them anywhere.'

The Perfect Fit

by Rachel Nolan

Thursday

They look back at me from the shop window, all shiny and new. Four inch heel and round toe. A gorgeous pair of shoes prescribes against anything. This is a rule I live by, and these lovelies will give me the confidence I need to get over the nerves of my first day on Monday. They're casual enough to wear as a day shoe but smart enough to give the right impression. Handing over my credit card, I distract myself so as not to see the amount on the screen, punch in my code and wait. The small white box with a gold panel across the front is placed on the counter in front of me. Strolling out of the shop, swinging my bag, I feel a little bit less anxious. My phone vibrates in my handbag and my mum's number appears on the screen. She never calls me before eleven in the morning.

I can't remember how I got there. I climb the stairs looking for directions etched on a wall somewhere. I hear my father's voice as I turn the corner and on hearing my footsteps he turns around. He looks like my father but somehow nothing like him. His eyes sink deep into a face unshaven and raw with emotion. I search his eyes for answers. He reaches over and puts his hand on my shoulder and I feel the weight of the words he can't say. I lean in and hug him. He smells like copper and fresh sweat, the way he always smells. I hug him tighter, trying to make a fresh memory and I'm suddenly aware of how long it's been since I told him I loved him.

He leads me to a room hidden at the back of the hospital and I open the door gently. My beautiful sister greets me with a smile but her eyes can't hide what her heart is feeling. I look towards my mother who is standing beside the bed, holding her hand.

I am a child again. My sister is a child. A horrible vision of a time when my mother won't be there crosses my mind. A time when she won't be there to hold my hand, and I will have to face the world without her. Watching her, my heart hurts from loving her so much. She holds my sister's hand, taking her pain and I look on and feel useless. I try to capture this moment of tenderness and to always remember what my mother was capable of. Then the realisation of what we have all lost hits me. My mother turns to me but I look away.

Friday

My sister's sobbing echoes through my parents' house. The grief lies. Heavy, thick, confusion. Voices sieve their way through the sadness. The kettle continually clicks as fresh tea is made. Chats around the kitchen table, feeling our way through the solitude, each one of us trying not to reach out and touch the other's pain.

I slide away to my room and lie on the bed. My white shoebox lies on the floor, mocking me. A shiver runs through me and stays. I reach for the duvet and bury myself beneath it, hoping to muffle my choking sobs.

Saturday

My mother creeps down the stairs, trying not to disturb a house of unsleeping people. I close my eyes and wait for someone else to get up first, unable to bear her haunted eyes just yet. My niece stirs and her chirping vibrates through the house. A shuffle of bodies and beds as everyone descends to the kitchen.

My father is the last one to come down the stairs and without speaking he walks over to my mother and leads her out to the car. They pull away and once again the kettle resumes its singing as we all sit waiting.

I hear my sister moving around in her room. I head back upstairs to help her as she decides what to wear. She searches through her collection of clothes but nothing is suitable. Everything is stretched out of shape and won't fit a body contorted with loss. She looks over at my shoebox and sighs heavily.

'It's the same size as that.'

'I know.'

She reaches over and traces the label with her finger. She lifts the lid and looks inside. Two sparkling new shoes lie side by side, snuggled together, a perfect fit.

'They're lovely.'

She says as she puts the lid back on and sits on the bed. I reach for a hairbrush and gently start brushing her hair. She strokes her empty, swollen belly and her eyes grow angry holding back the tears she refuses to let go of.

We hear the crunch of stones on the driveway as my parents arrive home.

My sister's fiancé comes in looking as detached as she does.

'It's time.'

He reaches for her hand.

The tiny casket is laid out on the bed, a small white box with a gold panel. My father reaches over and gently places the two tiny bodies together inside the box that should never have been made. He lays them side by side, snuggled together.

'They're a perfect fit.'

My father's first words since I came home. I watch as he lets the tears flow freely down his face.

Sunday

It's twelve before I can face the morning. Eager to rid myself of my own selfish grief, I quickly start gathering up my things. I look over at my new shoebox which lies discarded on the floor. I reach over, take out the shoes and start ripping up the empty box with a venomous rage that leaves me panting. I turn around and see my mother standing at the door. She walks towards me, picks up each piece of torn cardboard. She leans over and kisses me tenderly on my cheek, then turns and walks away. I throw my new shoes in my bag and leave, knowing I will never wear them.

Monday

I've always hated Mondays.

Compelled by Silence

I fight the need to steal the ideas of the writers around me while at the same time trying to clutch on to my own. I'd catch it if I dared to, dancing from one empty page to the other, meandering through the muddy words of each piece left unpolished, unfinished, never known. I have created space for my silences. The need to sit down and be still is a compulsion. My life has shaped itself in such a way that I allow for nothing but this to express what it is I haven't the courage to say. It touches me on my insides, past the flesh and past the bone.

Could the Devil Be Good?

According to believers, sins are the work of the devil. But if the devil punishes bad people, does this not make him good by virtue of his actions? I don't know if I believe in either and most of what I do know will serve me no purpose in the end. The only thing I can be sure of is that I know more than I did yesterday and less than I will know tomorrow. The rest is just the stuff that floods my empty pages.

Robert O'Brien

I've always been a daydreamer, a gift my parents encouraged in me. From them I gained other gifts, my father's love of history and my mother's passion for reading and Star Trek. In 1998 I made the decision to swap the concrete English jungle for the Forty Shades of Green, I wanted to know if the grass was truly greener on the other side. It was.

I indulge my love of history alongside good friends as part of an Irish military re-enactment group entertaining all over the country. I recently played a decidedly vile Black and Tan in the documentary The Valley Of Knockanure. Thanks to the Two Roads writing group I've found an outlet for the daydreaming soul, kindred spirits that I will never forget. I must also thank my two mentors on this journey who have quite literally changed my life.

I live in the shadows of the Comeragh Mountains. I am blessed to be married to an angel. Tracey, thanks for believing.

17

Morning

by Robert O'Brien

Silence. I'd forgotten what it was like to hear nothing. I close my eyes cutting myself off for a brief moment from the world around me, letting the sensation soak into my whole being. I'm reminded of my childhood, those seaside holidays my parents enjoyed so much. I, on the other hand, found them less than thrilling. Most children love the simple joys of sand and sea, lost in their own play filled worlds. But I would wade out into the sea at the first opportunity and submerge myself in its waters, desperate to escape from the revelry of the other beachgoers. It was the only way to drown out their noise. Even as a child I sought out solitude wherever I could find it. Some of my happiest memories are of walks in nature surrounded by the wonders of the world. My poor father thought I was a little odd. He may have been right. But eventually I learned to accept the inevitable. If you want to exist in the real world you have no choice but to play the game. You have to conform.

Birdsong. It cuts through the silence so suddenly that we all look up in the hope of catching a glimpse of wings above our heads. Its melody gentle and full of joy, so grotesquely out of sorts in this place. Then I hear the familiar sound of a bee as it drifts by, unaware of the world it travels through, intent only on its own needs. Somehow nature has found its way here against all the odds. Someone weeps openly beside me but I dare not look over. Instead I listen to the birdsong and my soul dances free. I am with her again, under the willow trees that grow in her parents' orchard, overcome with desire for the fruit of life. She is smiling and I touch her skin as only a lover can. She is my whole world, my reason for living. The thought of her brings a mixture of both joy and pain. I hold her image in my mind for as long as I can, soon it is time to return to the present.

Fear now replaces the fragile memory of courage. I take one final look at my watch. The bitter realisation of fate hangs over me; despair is my only companion. I stare transfixed by the watch, its hands moving dispassionately from one second to the next. I raise the whistle to my lips and take a last look at the others. They stare blankly back, not at me but at the whistle that trembles between my lips. The minute hand moves like the arrow of doom pointing to the end of the world. It is time.

The silence is gone, the birdsong ends. I pull myself up the ladder and stumble over the top of the trench. The others, their bayonets glistening in the morning sun, follow. We advance into the cauldron. The air now filled with the rattle of machine guns.

Heartbreaker

by Robert O'Brien

I open the door and the first thing that hits me is the smell, fried food and cheap coffee, the nectar of backstreet hovels. Once over the threshold I'm assaulted by the mob of voices from within, they're not spoken conversations but the chaotic ramblings of unrestricted thoughts. A tsunami of sound that threatens to engulf me in a myriad of human emotions pounding at my soul.

It has taken me a lifetime to come to terms with this gift. Control is the key. I visualise myself into the form of a sheep dog rounding up the voices, ushering them to a secure place within my mind, forcing them to do my bidding. I taught myself to do this during those dark, early years when they often threatened to overwhelm me.

I take a seat near the window, ignoring the sideways glances of the other patrons. I shroud myself in a veil of bland unimportance, robbing them of any memory of my arrival, another useful item from my mental bag of tricks. Not that I give a damn about these café folk one way or the other.

I start to sift through the voices while looking at the menu, its plastic cover smeared with greasy fingerprints and God knows what else. The waitress eventually appears at my table, her bored expression mirroring her casual thoughts. Her name is Claire. She feels trapped in this dead end job having to serve gutter trash day in day out. Sam, her boss, has been at her again. He's desperate for a quickie in the storeroom, no one need know he keeps telling her, but she'd know. I peek a little more into her soul and unlock something else. Eva, the pretty girl with the ocean blue eyes she met last week in the local library. I can feel her passion pulsing like a heartbeat of hope in a sea of dark emotions. I'm instantly overcome with jealousy.

I order a coffee and go back to the job at hand.

'You're slipping up, Jack,' the voice in my head says suddenly.

'I thought I told you never to call me at work,' I reply angrily. I feel embarrassed at being caught off guard by Him. Snooping around in people's thoughts for the Agency is one thing but doing it for my own gratification is quite another.

'You're getting jumpy in your old age Jack, you would never have let me sneak up on you like that in the old days.'

Robert O'Brien

'Can't you mind your own business for once?' I snap back.

'You're crowding my senses. I'll get back in touch when I've found our man.'

'Touchy today aren't we Jack? I can't help feeling that something's been bothering you lately?' I can almost see the smug grin on a face I've never actually seen in all the years that I have worked for Him.

'Jack?'

'This is my last job,' I say.

'I want my life back. I want to be able to wake up one morning without wondering if you'll pop into my head with another assignment. I want out.'

The voice is quiet.

'I think this is a conversation we should share off the clock, don't you Jack? Your target is male in his fifties, possibly a trucker who travels often and has a liking for young girls,' he adds finally without any hint of emotion.

'Is that it?' I'm surprised he's taken my desire to resign so calmly.

'Just get on with it, will you? Time is money.'

I take the hint. I let my mind drift free leaving only a thread of myself behind, anchored to my body; it is a lifeline that keeps me from drifting away. Then like a whisper instantly forgotten I touch their minds, one-by-one, gently brushing aside their outer thoughts until their inner most secrets are laid bare to me. It's no easy thing to immerse oneself into another's psyche. For a brief moment you become a part of them, you see through their eyes and feel their emotions as if they were your own.

I am a lonely widower called William, waiting for the day when I will see my beloved wife again. I have just bought the pills that I hope will help me achieve that very thing.

I am a teenage prostitute called Shelley, preparing myself for another evening of being used as a living toilet by men who sleep soundly beside their wives afterwards. I need the money for rent and my kids' school fees and a million other basic things that most people take for granted.

I am Jonathan; an English teacher in a boy's school, tormented by desires of the flesh that I know will see me fall from the path of decency. I have told a priest at confession about my secret, but a few Hail Marys won't save my soul from the pit.

I am Diana, a married mother of two, waiting for my husband's boss to whisk me off to his apartment. I love my husband, but I also know that I'm addicted to the sin I'm committing.

I am Daniel, an illegal immigrant, tortured by memories of the family

I left behind in Lagos. I know in my heart that they are dead. And I know that I am to blame.

I am Tara, a fourteen-year-old school girl with a head full of boys and a pack of cigarettes in my school bag.

I am Gus, a long distance truck driver with a gut full of food and I'm looking at the girl. Her skirt is just short enough to let me glimpse her perfect thighs and her blouse is thin and tight, just the way I like. I pull away with such force that I leave him stunned by the effort. He rubs at his temple and then looks around the café as if looking for the cause of his sudden distress.

'Too close Jack, he felt you,' the voice says with alarm.

'You have to deal with him. Now!'

I'm back in my self again. I look over at the target. His agitation clearly visible, I have to act fast before he leaves. When I entered his mind I saw the faces of dozens of young girls. He was a monster, like all the others the agency has sent me after. A freak of human nature with a heart colder than ice and a mind filled with hateful needs.

'Work your magic, Jack.' The voice adds like a proud father.

I slip into Gus again. He feels my assault but he can't understand what is happening. I fill his world with pain, tormenting every nerve in his body. The other patrons are suddenly aware of his discomfort but can only watch as his body is racked by convulsions. I have become his puppeteer and they are my audience. I rip into his mind and steal the identities of the girls he has stored away from the world. I record his vile crimes for the agency records. And then I move deeper. His heart is like a wounded animal fighting for survival, a truly terrifying thing to behold, but this is nothing new to me, I've been here before. My mind becomes a hand and it envelops the thrashing organ. I can sense his terror, he knows the end is coming. I begin to squeeze, quickly putting more pressure on. It tries to work, that's what it was designed to do, but I am its master now. I let him see me, his executioner, just for a split second. Then I finally crush it.

I slip out quietly during all the confusion.

'Not your best work Jack, a little too messy.'

'Maybe my heart isn't in it anymore,' I reply.

'Very funny. Now what was it you were talking about earlier, about leaving the agency?'

I feel a little pain in my chest but I let it pass. It's not good to dwell on things you can't control. Still the job got done and in the end that's all that matters.

The things I do for a pay cheque.

Reign of Silence

The sun is King over the heavens again. The guns have ceased their rain of hate. The battlefield now echoes with the desperate cries of the wounded and the dying. Men call for their wives and sons weep for mothers they will never see again. Yet I feel more alone at this moment than I have ever done before. I am lost in plain sight.

We came here in ranks of life, grasping weapons of power in our godlike hands. We, the sons of righteous men had come to bring justice to the ungodly. But here we lie, torn and broken on the butchered earth, our bright futures gone in the fog of what could have been. I wanted to marry and be a father, I wanted a million trivial joys to be mine in a life well lived. But now that has all been stolen from me by an enemy I have not even seen.

I think of the others that have fallen by my side. The doctors who will never heal, the farmers who will never sow their fields and the writers who will never create. This place is now the graveyard of more than just our flesh and bones.

Then silence reigns over everything. Silence. I strain my last reserves of life and listen to its emptiness. Am I alive or dead?

Peace arrives unannounced for a brief, beautiful moment. I welcome its touch and follow it. I am not alone anymore.

The guns begin again. The raised voices of men fill the air in a futile attempt to ward off death.

The second wave has begun.

The Silent Sin

The bible is filled with stories about sin. It tells us of the evils of temptation and how our faith in God is the only way to save our mortal souls. So why is it that we were born with it thrust upon us in the form of Original Sin? I can't help thinking that we were all doomed from the very moment we were born. The dictionary describes it as being the breaking of divine or moral law. I'm not sure about the divine part but it's the moral term that now tortures me.

I had always known that something was wrong, even back in the early days. But I chose to ignore the signs because he was my teacher, my mentor and most importantly my friend. He was a true paragon of virtue, well loved by his parishioners. That's why his betrayal was such a bitter pill to swallow.

I believed his affection for the boy to be no different than that of a father for his son, a pure emotion. And yet that dark cloud of doubt hung over me, constantly tugging at my soul. But still I did nothing.

Now he is gone to another parish far from the accusing eyes and whispered slander that echoes amongst the empty pews of this once proud place. His sin, like a cancer has eaten away at the faith of this community, leaving only cruel suspicion in its wake.

As for me, I must accept my part in his actions. I had the moral duty to protect my flock and in that I failed completely. In some ways I am as guilty as he is though my crime is the sin of silence.

Mairead Phelan

My father exported poultry and salmon. Timber boxes of
fowl and wildlife were sent to market mostly in England.
The feathers were also made use of especially the down.
I lived over a grocery and bar. The pub part had a snug
and was open only during shop hours. I even bought
fresh strawberries for a jam factory and saw blackberries
bought and put in barrels. I saw rabbits being skinned. I
wrapped turkeys for the post at Christmas. I learned Irish
at Ring College; attended two boarding schools and two
schools of nursing in Dublin. I milked cows and raised
four children who were under twelve years when their
father died. I look after some forestry and a small farm. I
like radio and scribbling.

18

It's All the Same in a Hundred Years

by Mairead Phelan

Billy Curtin is a secret only I know. This is his story.

4th May 1865. It was four o'clock this dark, cold morning when Billy Curtin prepared to leave the Rower, Co. Kilkenny to walk the five miles to the fair at Irishtown, New Ross, Co. Wexford, Ireland. The cattle lowed as Billy tried to open the frosty catch on the cattle byre. The gate lock was bound with frost as well. He walked the yearlings over the Ferry Bridge, the metal centre of which rattled noisily as they passed. There he met the 'Tangler' Murphy who tried to persuade him to sell but Billy knew from experience that if he persevered he would get a better price at the fair.

'What will you give me for these fine bullocks?'

'They're worth a pound I'd say.'

'Go away outa that,' said Billy. 'I might as well bring them home again for that price.'

Billy was confident, his blue eyes were intense. He was in charge of the situation. The 'Tangler' knew how to make a few extra pounds for himself on the resale. He would have to find another fool. With a few wallops of the stick the bullocks headed up the hill and in by

McMurrough's castle to the Irishtown.

If they did as well as the six fat cattle he sold last fair day he should have enough money for what he needed. Billy had a bag packed with some bread, bacon and provisions to feed him for the day.

He hoped his mother Rita hadn't noticed when she kissed him goodbye that he had collected a bag of clothes from an outhouse. These clothes hidden on a bullock's back contained priestly garb belonging to his uncle Fr Bob who had visited the previous year. It was handy for the priest to have spare clothes and vestments in his sister's house when he made the long journey home from South Carolina.

The fair was held on the first Tuesday of every month except the May 4th fair. This was the best fair of the year as cattle were expected to be in good condition by that time after the winter. All the buyers would be out in force this day.

Mary Grant, the love of Billy's life, had sailed on the Dunbrody for New York the previous April. He couldn't tolerate life around the Rower without her. Billy had had a lovely meal with Mary in Whelan's Eating House on the lane way from Quay Street to the post office before she left. He had relived every moment of that meeting, day and night since they had parted.

Billy's father Peter had more respect for the plough horses than Billy. The previous month he had taken the whip to Billy and his brother Jim when they left the horses standing out in the rain instead of inside the stable that evening. This had strengthened his resolve to join Mary.

The noise of cattle rose above the din of the market place; pigs squealed behind their creels and sheep bleated in makeshift pens, as farmers tried to huddle them together in case any made a rush for freedom. The inhabitants of the Irishtown had put up old doors or whatever as shutters on the windows, in case the cattle made a go for them as well. A woman was on the lookout with her scoop and bucket to collect the dung for her garden. Some had country relatives that would come well laden with eggs, potatoes or whatever they had to give to their kin. Family members were always welcome regardless of the circumstances.

Billy had a tough job getting the money from the jobber for his few cattle, but his persistence paid off. He had met him first at the crossroads at the Ferry Bridge. The cattle were sized up and a lower price than their value was offered. Billy knew not to pay heed to the buyers at this stage. A few meetings later the bargain was made.

'You'll give me a tanner luck money?' The jobber asked.

They spat on their hands and shook on it. The jobber asked Billy to drive the bullocks across the bridge where the drover collected them and took them to the Quay of Waterford for a boat trip to England. He then had to march the cattle, down the High Hill, across the river by the New Ross Bridge. His heart was light at this stage as all was going according to plan.

Billy found a wall behind which he changed into his priestly garb. Then he walked fifty yards on to the shipping office to book a ticket for the Dunbrody. He had no problem booking a passage as a priest. Billy had only to remember to keep calm and behave like one. He had always been at Fr Mullin's beck and call. He might not be expected to say Mass on the ship, as he had no chalice or vestments. He prayed God would forgive him the sacrilege. He looked over the passengers booked in and there was no name familiar to him. Next stop he hoped would be New York. The ship had pulled in to berth on the quay earlier that week with a load of timber from Newfoundland for Graves Timber Merchants Ltd, New Ross. It was all unloaded now and the ship was ready to sail on the tide. There was not a full complement of passengers aboard so it left New Ross to go up the Irish Sea en route for Liverpool.

Mary Grant left Ireland in April 1864 with her parents. Graves Timber Merchants owned the Dunbrody and were agents for the Canada Company. The latter gave out grants of land to emigrants from Ireland. Billy's only letter from Mary was full of news. She gave him details of how to reach her if he came after her as he had hinted he might.

Quebec, Canada
July 1864
Dearest Billy,

We have settled in Canada near Quebec. The land we were granted is 1000 acres of trees. We harvest at least three different kinds of mushrooms and berries e.g. Juniper. The land runs down to the St Lawrence River where fish are large and plentiful. Mother is a great cook. We can smoke or salt the salmon, whiting or whatever the good Lord sends. We have to be careful and bring out the shotgun as there is an occasional black bear lurking around. We found wild honey in a tree nearby so we are certainly well fed. Harry Sutton, the man who previously owned the land, is tutoring us in the ways of the forest and we look after him as he is beginning to get feeble. He had a log cabin homestead in need of repair, so Dad being a carpenter is in his element fixing it up for us all. It is well insulated with shingle slates, we all live with him. He had no family so he made us very welcome. I miss you so much. I can be reached by sending a letter by Graves and Co. Ltd, to the Canada Company. The crossing was fairly smooth for us although Mother was a little seasick at first.

All my love,
Mary

Billy had forgotten this letter when rushing for the fair but the words were written on his heart.

Rita, Billy's mother, was distraught when Billy didn't return. She had three other sons and four daughters but the family had always been close knit. Rita searched Billy's room that night. She found a letter under his pillow from Mary. The following day his few possessions including the letter and anything that reminded her of Billy were assigned to the bottom of a tin chest in the attic. Rita would devote her time to her other children. That was her firm decision. Billy's actions were not to be glorified in case they would follow suit. Rita's hair turned grey the year after he left. She died five years later and his possessions were never discussed or brought out. Her daughter Susan carried on the family tradition of not referring to Billy. Susan in turn had her daughter Molly. The secret turned over with the generations, everyone keeping the silence.

Molly grew up to find love with Jack Harris. He was helping at a neighbour's threshing when he first saw her and she first saw him. He was a fine cut of a lad with blond hair and deep blue eyes. He seemed quiet and wise. He couldn't take his eyes off her that night at the house dance. Jack told her he'd meet her when she was selling eggs in the local grocery shop in New Ross. He knew she went to town on Tuesdays. That Tuesday was the beginning of a new time, a new generation. They were to have many decades of happiness. Over the years Jack came to know her. He loved the way her face smiled all the time. The corners of her mouth usually seemed to be suspended upwards by the grooves from the side of her nostrils, but now and then when she was tired they drooped. Now she seemed more than tired. Now she seemed a bit down. Over the years he prised it out of her. Molly wondered what happened to her Uncle Billy. He hadn't been heard of since he left in 1865. Her mother Susan hadn't mentioned him in the house for years. Grandmother Rita had thought Mary Grant, the woman he had fallen in love with, wasn't good enough for him at all. Not knowing what had happened to him ate Rita up inside. He hadn't contacted his uncle, Fr Bob, either who would have forgiven him everything. The feeling of loss was something all the family felt, though no one knew why it was thought that it was best to keep their name intact and their home place unblemished.

'God bless me and me wife,
Our son Dick and his wife,
Us four no more
Now and forever more Amen.'

The rhyme hinted at the loyalty that ran deep in the family. Molly stuck to their tradition. She inherited her grandmother's being so proud. She also never spoke of her Uncle Billy again. They never did anything wrong in her bloodline. If they did, it wasn't to be mentioned outside.

When Jack and Molly had settled at the bottom of the hill, fifty one years previously, the place seemed like heaven on earth. The green valley stretched out below to the river. In the morning sunlight it was still a sight to see through the few oak trees of the house field. Even heaven has secrets. They would never find out about the disgraceful conduct of their Uncle Billy. Not from her anyway. Any skeletons in the cupboard should be left there. That had been Rita, Susan and Molly's policy. They seldom mentioned this black sheep of an uncle. Now more than a hundred years later no one seemed to care. It took another generation dying out for long ago's story to be told.

Two generations after Rita had secreted them away, Billy's remaining possessions were resurrected by Molly. As Susan lay dying she told Molly where to find the belongings.

'Billy was my favourite brother. I was sorry not to have made my peace with him.'

Molly left that deathbed with the resolve of finding the peace her mother and grandmother had been deprived of. In turn she looked for the guidance of her own granddaughter, Anna, to help resolve a conflict that had died with Susan, but had not been forgotten by the family. Four generations after Rita lost her son, Anna, a beautiful child of ten years, helped to find him. A ten year old had the skills to find out what had happened over a hundred years before. She was a whiz kid on the internet and Molly was excited as she gave her information. She instructed her granddaughter to look up a person who seemed to have vanished once he left New Ross. The details were sketchy given the secrecy around his disappearance and his mother's refusal to refer to him again. Billy Curtin was at a fair in New Ross and never came home. It was suspected he went off on the Dunbrody. Molly asked Anna to search for Billy in New York records as well as New Ross ones. In a few button presses, Anna uncovered a history no one else in the family knew, but Molly had some inkling of. There on the screen, the facts lay in recorded entries of embarking and disembarking. She couldn't believe her eyes. Her suspicions were correct. The records were kept in New York unlike those in New Ross. It was there in black and white on the screen that Bill Curtin left as a priest on the Dunbrody. Anna's great-grand Uncle Billy's deception of more than one hundred years ago had been definitely uncovered. Molly wondered whether he had any descendants. That would take some more research.

Making contact with the past brought the past to meet the present. Molly contacted Graves and Co., business associates of the Canada Company. By enquiring at the Canadian Embassy Molly found an address and phone number for an owner of land granted in 1864. Molly realised that life was short, so she phoned that number in Canada on St Patrick's morning.

'Hello,' a man answered.

The line was so clear she might as well have been talking to a neighbour.

'Hello,' Molly said, 'Is this the Grant household?'

'William Curtin speaking.'

Taken aback by the simplicity of connecting she said:

'I could be your cousin from Ireland, my uncle Billy Curtin left

'My grandfather was Billy Curtin,' he said. 'I remember him longing to make contact before he died.'

'That's right,' Molly replied. 'My mother was just the same. It's all the same in a hundred years.'

William had an email address. Anna, her granddaughter with no living recollection of the lost son, set her up with one too. Molly and William corresponded at length over the next few days.

Molly found out that Billy married Mary shortly after he arrived in Canada. The world was too small a place for him and he hadn't enough to occupy himself. His father in law, Mary Grant's father, who had just lost his wife, got involved in minding Billy's grandchildren. Then Billy left for the Klondike. He became a Klondiker in his fifties and returned at fifty-five a rich man having found gold to share with his family. He could have afforded a trip home at any stage but he couldn't face the prospect. The son Rita was ashamed of would have made her more proud than any of her children.

He lived to almost a hundred years with good health to the end.

Elvis on Sin

Men can tell lies about love to get their way with gullible young girls. Elvis in the song says, "It's a sin to tell a lie". I know women can lie as well perhaps without blinking an eye. He continues, "Millions of hearts have been broken". It seems to have been a sin in the past. Elvis thought it was a sin anyway. He sings again, "Shall I stay? Would it be a sin?" It seems it was a sin to love someone in twentieth century Ireland. Sin was often talked about at retreats. I think now no one knows what a sin is. I learned that three things were necessary for a mortal sin: free will, full knowledge and a grave matter. Now I wonder who decides? God I hope, but you have to believe in a God for this to work. Otherwise one can sin away. Carry on regardless!

Valerie Ryan

What a life it's been so far. I work as a journalist. I spent my childhood playing in the lush tobacco fields of Canada - but I don't smoke. Finding Spain was like a second home; learning to fly, and running a restaurant in Wicklow with my husband, the late John Kerr, will always be a source of fun and adventure for writing and stories. Expanding from journalism life into tutoring, both in literacy and creative writing, has been another rich curve. Co writing *It's a Small World* for adult learning was, for me, a great education; treasuring time among the stunning hills and fields of Wicklow and Kildare is the perfect background for creative inspiration.

19

The Perfect Customer
by Valerie Ryan

She gazed at the shoes as their owner slid into the chair. Brush and pan in hand, she stifled the urge to flick off a speck of mud on the toe of one shoe. They were handmade, elegant and discreet. Reversing out from under the table she looked up at the man wearing them. The rest of the outfit was a brown suit in a fine weave, which looked soft to the touch but held its shape firmly. The cut fell perfectly from the shoulders, causing no wrinkles on the material as it hung. The man had a newspaper half opened ready to read.

He gave her a quick look.

'Coffee,' he turned to his newspaper adding without looking up, 'very hot and strong.'

That's how it was every Tuesday at around 11.10 am.

She always scalded the cup before she made that coffee. Sometimes he smiled. Well, his mouth smiled, but the granite coloured eyes stayed constant and she wondered what he'd do if the coffee were cold.

Some days, he wore different suits and other shoes, but the brown were her favourites. Where you found such suits was beyond her. Perhaps they were made abroad. The man certainly had taste.

He slipped into table five at the back, which no one ever wanted because you couldn't see out the window. From the other tables you could see out onto a lovely garden across the road. All you could see from table five was the front door. He appeared usually at 11.11 am or

11.12 am and she dropped whatever she was doing just before 11.10 am, to scald his cup and have the machine ready to go.

He never brought a mobile phone or met anyone else. He sat and flicked through two or three newspapers for five minutes and left. Never varying a detail in his visits, he never chatted or made any personal contact. She was ashamed to admit to herself that she was apprehensive telling him the price of the coffee had gone up. When she did he looked irritated. All he did was nod and then left too much money on the table to save further comment.

Each Tuesday for six months he arrived, sat at table five and drank his coffee in his impeccable suits and elegant brogues. When one Tuesday came and went with no sign of him, she pictured him in Barbados in a tailored linen suit and casual handmade loafers with an equally elegant wife who did what she was told.

That evening she was just starting to peel and chop the carrots and the onions for Wednesday's soup while Thomas peeled the potatoes in the back kitchen. He had fixed up a television out of sight of the customers to watch a rerun of his latest appearance as a corpse in a popular soap. While he waited for jobs in acting he waited on tables for her. Suddenly, Thomas called out 'Come quick.' She saw the eight o'clock news was on.

'Today, businessman Carlos Hunt, also known as Carl Hunt, is to face charges of defrauding his partner,' said the reporter. 'But Hunt's partner has disappeared and his whereabouts are unknown. There are fears that the case will be dismissed as soon as it reaches this courtroom.' He said 'dismissed' with a great flourish.

'So what?' She said, shrugging her shoulders at Thomas.

Thomas stabbed at the air towards the screen. She glanced back and caught her breath. The man, Hunt, was caught on camera walking towards the court. Looking at one another, disbelieving, neither said a word. It was the elegant man in the brown suit and the brown shoes.

She admired how well he looked on television. Respectable and smart, she thought, but he kept his grey eyes down. Then, just as suddenly, he was gone from the screen and Thomas was mouthing an exaggerated 'Wow!'

He looked crestfallen when she said indifferently:

'We've lost a regular, that's for sure'. Turning on her heel she hurried back into the kitchen and, walking as far as the doorway she glanced into the darkened coffee shop and shuddered. She chewed her lip and returned to the back kitchen and the vegetables, chopping over and over until they resembled crumbs.

Two months later, one Tuesday at 11.07 am Hunt slipped back to his favourite table. Caught unawares she added up imaginary sums once or twice on the calculator until she pulled herself together. She didn't dare to look over. Scalding a cup, she got on with making his coffee and taking a deep breath dropped it over.

They heard nothing about Hunt since they had seen him on television. She glanced over almost unwillingly while he drank his coffee. Nothing had changed. If he thought they had seen the publicity about the case, he was unperturbed. Later that day she searched for 'Carlos Hunt' on the web. All charges had been dropped in a case against the businessman. The story added that he was the son of a Spanish mother and Canadian father. His career took off when he married a well known socialite and ran her father's company even when they divorced. She died in a car accident and he married an actress briefly until divorcing her too. The business partner he was supposed to have defrauded never reappeared, and had been the State's only witness for the prosecution. She read it again. Leaning back in the chair she went to slam the laptop shut and halted, her hand poised in mid air. Instead she brought her hand down slowly and closed it with careful deliberation. He did not become a regular again.

For about six months she watched the door on Tuesdays at 11 am until one week it didn't strike her until Wednesday morning, and she was very pleased she hadn't thought about him once.

One Tuesday morning, Hunt slipped back into his seat and spread out his newspaper. She splashed boiling water onto her thumb as she scalded the cup and grimaced. After she dropped the coffee over she hurried to run cold water on her hand in the kitchen. Seconds before he left another man came in. Small and muscular, he seemed to be tripping along on his toes rather than the flat of his feet. He came up to the counter and bought a sandwich.

'I think I know that guy the one who's just gone out. Do you know his name?' She said nothing so he tried again. 'Is he a regular? Does he always come in at this time?'

Getting no answers, he headed for the door. Watching him through the window, she saw he flicked the sandwich into the bin outside. The door opened and another man entered. His eyes took in everyone inside, lighting on every detail. This was not a customer but not a health inspector. They only looked for dirt. This man looked at everything. He approached the counter.

'Are you the manager?' He asked finally.

'Yes, can I help?' She feigned politeness.

'Can we talk?' He motioned her to one side.

Clutching the serving cloth she sat down with him in the quiet corner. He showed his identification: Tim Harding. Detective Special Finance Taskforce.

'Just to let you know I've been liaising with the UK authorities on a fraud case which may involve one of your regular customers.' Watching her, he paused but she said nothing. 'I need to know who works here.' This time he waited until she said something.

'Just me and Thomas.'

'Thomas who?'

'Thomas Ferguson.'

'Anything to Alex?' He tried to coax a smile.

'Alex? The football manager? No, he isn't,' was all she volunteered.

'As I came in a small sandy haired man was outside. I think he had been in here. Had he?'

'A small squat sort of man? Tough looking. Yes.'

'Do you know him?'

'No. Never seen him before today.'

'Does the name Carl or Carlos Hunt mean anything to you?'

'Carl Hunt?' she repeated and her voice was cautious now.

He waited again and his mouth tightened slightly.

'I understand Carlos Hunt is a customer here. Is that right?'

'I don't know a lot of the customers' names. There was a guy on the news about two months ago called Carlos Hunt and, yes, he used to come in on Tuesdays.'

'Did the tough guy ask about Hunt?'

'Yeah. How did you know?'

He looked at her for a minute. 'I'll be in next week and, whatever happens, please go on with everything you normally do.'

'Should we close next Tuesday?' She sat up very straight as she asked.

'That is not going to happen,' Harding told her, dropping his card on the table before leaving to go, and added, 'See you Tuesday.'

He was as good as his word. Appearing shortly after she opened up the detective melted into the background as just another customer. About five minutes before 11 am the stockily built man appeared.

'Thomas. Customer,' she used a vaguely sing song voice.

He sat down and Thomas went over to him.

'Say, Thomas?' She called quietly when he finished serving. 'It might be a good time to get change while we're quiet? And after the bank, could you get some heads of lettuce, please?' She pulled out a fifty euro note from the till, passed it to him and he left.

Right on cue Hunt arrived. Slipping in without looking left or right, he sat at table five. There were only two regulars having breakfast at a table by the window and they were discussing racing, oblivious to all else. She dropped two scones and they rolled out from behind the counter. They made her think of grenades.

Hunt drank his coffee and scanned his papers. No one else arrived. The tough little man barely drank his and looked at the paper in front of him, but his eyes didn't move across the page. She had almost forgotten Harding who was working through a crossword. She drew a triangle to keep her hand steady and traced over it several times. Pressing into the paper, she stopped at each point to glance at the men in turn without lifting her head.

Eleven minutes passed and Hunt stood to go. Stocky Man stiffened but did not move from his chair. Instead of leaving the money on the table, Hunt turned in the direction of the counter, as he walked he put his hand inside his jacket. Standing still, holding two dirty cups in her hand, she watched, horrified. There was little room between the tables. There was an irritating scraping sound of chairs as Hunt stumbled, steadying himself on the back of Stocky Man's chair. Finally, he was at the counter placing the precise change down he left quickly. Reacting instantly, Stocky Man was on his feet. He started to turn from the table as the door closed but crashed back on to the floor. Clutching his chest he shuddered as his breath came in tight gasps.

The two regulars at the window were up but Harding was there first. Kneeling by the body, he gestured for them to stay put as he talked into a phone.

'Yes. Ambulance. Now.' She heard him say. She put down the cups and went over to the door peering out.

An ambulance was there in a jiffy and she wondered if it had been on standby. Harding calmly reassured the two customers that he had everything under control. She waved them on and so they hurried out. Once the ambulance moved off, Harding called back in from the door to ask if she was all right? She said she was, he added that he would call another day but all she said was,

'No, don't I'll be fine.'

She was, the welcome routine settled back and she was more than happy with the small day to day dramas.

The weeks passed and she never mentioned the events to Thomas; sometimes she thought she should but he was so busy auditioning that his cousin filled in for him most of the time. In the end she decided to change table five to a new, admittedly tighter, space farther out on the floor.

She was clearing the crumbs after the breakfast rush one Tuesday morning when the door opened. At 11.10 am her favourite brown shoes walked across the floor; there was a slight hesitation as Hunt looked around and found table five in its new spot.

The Heaviness of Silence

There is no talking now. But people are at their loudest. Focused, scratching pens. Thinking. Attention flicking in and out of the room. The first floor above weighs down on us, so heavy and so silent. Only murmuring reaches from another room. The wind is pushing relentlessly at the doors and windows trying to prise them open. Each time it gets in, it celebrates with a whistle.

Sinning in Moderation

We watch out for it, we know it, we punish it, we do it and we confess it. We are entertained by sin, enraged by sin and baffled by sin. Sinning, like everything, is good for us in moderation. As sinners, we'll never have to throw the first stone. It's only after we are sinned against that we choose to sin less. It's only then we learn that too much sin rots the soul.

Steven Thomas

I am excited by writing and the opportunities opening up to me. Having shown an interest in writing at an early age I am delighted to be returning to a former love. I draw on past experiences at home and abroad to give my unique view on the frailties of people I have met and dreamed I have met. Nothing surprises me anymore and I feel somehow responsible for the mess the country is in as a result of never voting! I hate the way the world is laughing at Ireland and look forward to bouncing back and showing them what a great country and people we are! I am married to the gorgeous Suzanne and am lucky to have friends and family close to hand. My only wish is to be happy and maybe get four more years of playing football before my knees finally give up!

20

The Cherry Picker

by Steven Thomas

It was my cousin Danny who finally brought me up to see her. If there was anything dangerous or illegal going on in my life when I was fifteen or sixteen, he was the instigator. From stealing hubcaps to knocking over a 7 Eleven or giving me my first beer and smoke of a joint, Danny was the one at my side. Ma said Danny O'Brien could sweet talk the devil just like his dad. But all the sweet talking in the world wasn't going to get his father out of a fifteen year stretch for armed robbery. It's twenty years to the day that Danny brought me up to Queens to see the cherry picker and it still seems like yesterday.

Danny O'Brien wasn't my real cousin, like, his Da and my Da weren't brothers. They were cousins, so we were like second cousins but that was enough for Danny. When he brought me the first time to meet his gang, they could sense straight away that I wasn't like them. I kinda liked the buzz to get into trouble just as much as they did but because I was doing all right at school they never trusted me. Danny fought my corner but then he'd let me fight my own battles too and sometimes against him. He pointed out to the gang that I had brains to burn and could always think up something smart on the spot. And when I started using my smarts for the gang's benefit I slowly got accepted. When we knocked over the sports store because I sweet talked the young assistant into getting in a tent with me that was the making of me! And I was fast too. There was never any way I would ever be caught in a chase and if caught you never rat on a friend - say nothing! Da said I took after my mother's brother Vincent who'd run like the wind anytime he'd get some broad stuffed. But in truth I was always on the edge of the group and I suppose that was my place and it was fine with me. I still got to run with the gang who had built up quite a reputation for themselves in Brooklyn by the turn of the nineties.

If Danny needed a place to stay he'd rap on my window and stay, especially if one of his mother's boyfriends were acting the dick, which turned out to be nearly every other night. He hated his mother for what she was doing when his old man was doing time but she was a junkie and junkies don't have time for family. When he'd stay over that's when Danny would let his guard down. He was the most naturally funny guy I had ever met. So full of fun and devilment. But when we were with the gang he could be both downright vicious and violent to me. That was the nature of the beast you had to have your game face on. Once you were in a gang you had to put up or else you were swallowed up and spat out. Danny was the leader. Always on his toes to prove to all he was the toughest and meanest. I remained on the edge, barely clinging on to the gang's shirttails.

On the shirttails you get to see everything. I got to see the night when the huge black kid from the Bronx pulled a blade on Danny. I didn't like what I saw. It all suddenly got very real. Like, we were fighting. But it was a game. It was a game up until Danny decided to end it. Everyone from the two rival gangs just stopped fighting with each other and looked at the scene unfolding. The big kid from the Bronx just smiled at Danny and nodded at him. I looked at Danny's face and couldn't believe there was no fear in his eyes. He actually looked delighted. Danny just reached into his jacket pocket and pulled out a gun. He did not say a word. The kid from the Bronx nodded his head again. This time his smile was one of fear. Like a cornered mutt! He put his blade away, turned tail and ran. We chased his gang down the tracks, kicking their asses as they ran, Danny leading the way as they scurried back to their holes in the Bronx.

We partied hard that night. Danny had got a load of dope to sell as well as the imitation gun from one of his mother's boyfriends. I think this latest one was white!

But Danny had stepped it up a gear. There were no more petty crimes. Now it was cars getting stolen not just the hubcaps. Now it wasn't just cans of beer and smokes knocked off from the 7-Eleven. It was the takings and bottles of Jack. In a short space of time even dope wasn't good enough. I heard rumours the gang was dealing in harder shit now. I say the gang because by this stage I had been frozen out. There was never anything formal or an incident which led me to being kicked out. It was kind of gradual and it was all Danny's doing. He didn't need to stay over anymore now. His mother's boyfriend was well connected and Danny O'Brien was making a name for himself and going places fast. The cops had even stopped calling at my door. You know you're something else when your parents wonder why the cops aren't calling.

School started again and I had a big year ahead. Teachers told my Ma that if I kept my grades as they were, kept my nose clean this year and kept running as fast for the school team I'd get a scholarship for sure. So my parents came down hard and banned Danny. Not that they needed to. I never saw him anymore but I heard of his exploits, especially through his cousin Patricia who I'd started seeing. She was tall like all the women on Danny's mother's side. She had jet black hair and those dewy eyes you could be forgiven for thinking you were in the company of an angel.

It was the last week of September the day before my sixteenth birthday when I'd been drinking some cans at home as my parents were gone out for the day. I was pissed because I just had a fight with Patricia on the phone so I started walking into town looking for some trouble. I heard a call from behind me.

'Hey Dopey! It's your birthday today my Ma was telling me!' Danny roared from the car he was driving. Trouble had just found me. 'Jump in! It's about time you visited the cherry picker!'

So I jumped. Danny pulled over to a phone box to make the call. With the sleeveless T shirt Danny was wearing I could see he had added a couple more tattoos to his collection. After finishing the call he stopped to chat up some cute thing walking by. Number got and we were driving up to Queens. I knew what was ahead of me.

Danny started teasing me about being a virgin and how I hadn't nailed his cousin. That everyone had. I knew that was bullshit because if a fifteen-year-old put out like he said she did it would be common knowledge. Anyways the stories from the gang were the cherry picker was a bored housewife whose husband worked shift. Not only would she let you have sex with her she would pay you for the honour. Of course not everyone was allowed otherwise every dog from the Tri State would be sniffing around. No, the catch was that she only liked boys who were not quite men – virgins! She liked picking our cherries and we pretended to like giving them to her. But how do you know you're gonna like it?

The story was legendary especially in the bars where working men had to pay hard earned money to nail some ass. Young guys getting paid to nail some woman. You could not make it up. Danny's gang had stumbled across her and kept her to themselves which was reasonable as you didn't want everyone knowing about this sweet little earner. They had not gone out in ages because she didn't like when they came in stoned or fall down drunk and the buzz of it had worn off for them.

Now it was my turn, I never thought I'd get around to it and was never that bothered. Now I was outside her door and no turning back.

'Don't get cheeky, she'll throw you out,' Danny had warned me on the way over.

Danny got out and left me waiting in the car. I would follow when he gave the sign.

I could not make her out from the car but it looked like her and Danny were arguing. Danny signalled furiously for me to come on. I closed the car door and ran up the garden path as quickly as I could. Closing the door behind me I saw Danny standing in the hall.

'Now remember Dopey, no smart shit!'

I followed him into the living room where there was a big television playing MTV. Danny shoved me into sitting on the sofa next to Cherry Picker. I had a quick look at her but without really looking at her. She was tall, about forty, but could have been any age and no oil painting! I suddenly realised that I was really nervous and was kind of shivering even though there was sweat running down my back.

'So Danny, who do we have here?' The cherry picker rubbed a finger along her bottom lip and seemed to purr the last word.

'It's Dope...my cousin Francis. He's still a virgin! Danny barely stopped himself in time from saying my hated nickname.

'So Francis, pleased to meet you. I'm Joanna and what age are you?'

'I'm fourteen...'

'He's fifteen, he will be sixteen tomorrow, Joanna!' Danny was clenching his fist and gritting his teeth. I kept thinking of the black kid's smile when Danny pulled the gun.

'So Francis I hope I'm not going to have any trouble with you, now am I?' With that she placed her hand on my crotch and squeezed ever so tightly.

'No, no Joanna! I'm sorry!' My voice squeaked and wavered.

This gave Danny great joy.

'Follow me!' Joanna stood up and walked out of the room.

Stunned, I stood to do as I was told but Danny was up like a light and shoved me back down on the sofa.

'I'm not doing your sloppy seconds Dopey!' Danny laughed as he took the stairs three at a go. I poured myself some juice, ate some biscuits and turned up MTV as it started getting noisy upstairs. Danny came down a while later, just wearing his socks carrying the rest of his clothes and sweating like a pig.

'Up you go Dopey! Give it to her good and don't let me down!'

I sprung up and took the stairs as Danny did, knocked at the bedroom door and waited until she answered before going in. Now to tell the truth I don't remember much of what went on in the cherry picker's bedroom. It's strange I know I was kind of drunk but I can clearly remember the clothes I was wearing that day because I couldn't take off my Doc Marten boots and had to shuffle over to the bed with my pants pulled down. I ripped off my Sonic Youth T shirt and threw it behind me. All I can say about the act, at first I was like a misinformed Labrador but with some coaxing and subtle hints I got into the rhythm of things. I really never looked her in the eye at all, I recall she had nice legs, no chest and wore sexy stockings!

I kept going for a while but before I knew it I was back out in the car heading for Brooklyn. The cherry picker had given Danny twenty bucks for calling over. I had now sold my virginity to this woman for ten bucks. Still, turning sixteen and paid to lay someone. I thought I was pretty much the shit. We drove around laughing and making stops that Danny had to do. When finished Danny brought me to a bar and talked with the owner before I was allowed in. The bar was dark and loud and Danny brought me down to the back where I recognised his mother's boyfriend and some of the gang. When I walked down to them they all cheered and picked me up and whooped and slapped my back. Every time I turned back from talking with someone there was another shot or beer in front of me. Soon I was in the toilets puking my guts up but I was still good to go.

When I walked out of the toilets I was greeted by a loud cheer again.

'Tell me I'm the best you ever had!' Danny roared in my face.

The whole place erupted. Danny must have been listening at the door of the cherry picker's bedroom the whole time. After being guided and directed by her I had started getting a little cocky.

I was still horrified. Danny came over with the others and patted me on the back again. The drinks and some smoke started going again and the next thing I know I was being woken up on my porch by my mother's slippered foot and sweeping brush the next morning.

The beating from my Pa was nothing towards the fear of Patricia finding out about my little secret. I met her at the park and couldn't hide my fear.

'Jesus, Francis what's up with you today?' Her face was angelic and innocent. My sordid news was going to destroy her forever. I couldn't hold back I just let it all out. I stood back expecting a left hander and the flood works to open. She barely flinched.

'Is that all? I thought it was something important. At least you won't be bothering me then!'

I wasn't so sure about her innocence anymore. She proceeded to tell me the story of how her and her friend Martha used to ring up a local perv and talk dirty to him. He would leave money out for them which they would use for clothes and jewellery! Within a day I had learned two valuable lessons from two different women. First I was so good at sex that I should be paid for it and second it is always better to come clean even if it is admitting to bedding a forty-year-old the night before.

I never got to see Danny alive again. I think the cherry picker was his way of saying goodbye. He got caught making one of his trips in his stolen car and was sent to Juvenile. Not long after he got out, a failed robbery got him to see his father up in the state penitentiary on an ongoing basis. Trouble was he also got to meet up with that big black kid from the Bronx and this time Danny didn't have a gun on him.

Standing at Danny's grave on my thirty-sixth birthday with tears of sorrow and joy it all could have been yesterday or it may never ever have happened at all.

The Harsh Word

There is no such thing as silence. Of course the tree makes tremendous noise when it crashes down in the deep forest. You might be able to enjoy a quiet moment or some down time at best. But a word of warning, if you do find yourself in the midst of enjoying luxurious quiet time do not make the mistake of allowing the word silence drift across your mind's eye. Because silence belies its very meaning. It is a loud, harsh and overrated word that conjures up images of ugly people looking down long noses over half finished glasses.

It Took Three People to Sin

It used to take only three people to sin. One had to commit the sin, another to be sinned against and finally the last person to judge the foul deed. Nowadays we have still the sinner, the sinned against but the media has taken on the role of judge, jury and executioner. Once a weapon of the Church, sin is very much a media whore.

Let he who is without sin cast the first stone. Anyways, sinning for me is outdated, it died with the Church. There are only right or wrong and grey areas thankfully open to misinterpretation and exploitation.

Mark Turner

I've pedalled the pushbike of life through the Shires' rolling hills, along the folded rocks of Scotland's lochs and out west to the fractured reaches of North Wales. Love found me in MacGillycuddy's Reeks. The Swiss Alps cured me of obsessive compulsion and yielded progeny.

Misfits, rogues and psychopaths take form in The Baptist and other works. Their voices, they speak to me. I have pleaded with them, but the demons are real.

I like all kinds of music and body painting.

21

Extract from The Baptist

by Mark Turner

Pinned down

Ray used to sit on my chest. I remember once in particular; the first time I saw his glow. A roasting summer's day, playing football with Ray and his friends on a large green. Ray had the friends, not me. One of those magical afternoons that last forever. Goals galore on both sides sent sailing between the makeshift goalposts. Time stood still. I wore the watch. My lack of athleticism offered the least danger of smashing it on the hard baked earth beneath the weedy grass. I noted the slow movement of the minute hand. Such days are golden when you're young. I have endured many subsequently. God knows it's the drugs.

Ray had scored a glorious goal. As he soared up the field, arms spread wide like an albatross, I hugged him and we fell to the ground in celebration. Rolling me onto my back he tore at the grass around us and scattered it over my hair, face and neck. I caught his infectious laughter. Eyes squeezed tight against the dust, I felt the grass falling between my teeth. I sensed the sun frame him. Then a lone cloud covered the sun, but his red halo remained, burning through my lids. Ray's knees were a bit painful on my biceps as he bounced his weight on my ribs. I felt the bones flex.

How easily I could have thrown him off. I was three years older and weighed more. Now I'm thirteen years older than him.

A few years later and he would have been my physical superior, with an athlete's shoulders and the thick wrists of a strongman. Even at eleven he was no pushover at arm wrestling. I was *Mister Weedy No Friends*, according to my little brother and his mates. But I had mathematics on my side. No, I don't mean some complex equation of leverage that would continue to overcome Ray's growing physical prowess. I'm talking of superior knowledge, algebra, calculus. That was, is, my forte.

My lack of friends and perpetual scowl worried Mum. She said I was depressed. Dad said it was normal teenage behaviour and I would soon discover girls, make friends, play sport, build muscles, drink beer and all that sort of thing. He was scared stiff I'd turn out to be gay. *Poof* is what people used to say in those days. *Homosexual* meant deviant and was too embarrassing a word to utter. I wasn't totally without macho pursuits, being an active member of a school karting club that appreciated my precision with all things mechanical. But Dad was convinced my preference for neat creases down the front of my denims was a sure sign of deviancy. That he should say that, the ancient deviant. My sexuality turned out to be the least of his concerns.

Ray was always pulling my chain, teasing me about how successful he was in the school rugby team and the fact that girls were already asking him to discos. Eventually I would snap, which made him laugh. He still smirked as I punched him, the halo growing stronger, feeding off my anger. Ray knew there wasn't enough strength in my skinny arms to really hurt him. So I tried to kick him in the balls, but Mum caught us and imposed a below the belt moratorium.

One day, soon after the never ending soccer match, it became too much to bear. Dropping the sporting taunts, he went for my dick. No, not an outlawed wrestling hold, but verbally. Ray said his was bigger than mine, which I'm ashamed to say it was, and further his friends thought my inferior appendage was indicative of me probably being a poof.

I paraphrase. He didn't say *inferior appendage* or *indicative*. Adult vocabulary was my province, along with the maths.

So I sat on Ray's chest, pinned his arms with my knees. He looked up in disbelief as I leaned forward to push deep muscle pain through his burgeoning biceps. I felt the flesh squelch against the eleven-year-old bones of his upper arms.

'Okay, squirt.' That was my pet name for him. 'If X squared equals two Y plus Z, and Y equals two Z, then what are the values of X, Y and Z? You have no idea what I'm talking about do you? You're a thicko, Ray, thick as a plank!'

There was no way he could push me off. Even without the weight difference it would have been difficult for him to get up. Mock sun blazed upon his head. Yes, he strained with those talented footballer's feet, even arched his back slightly off the bottom of the bathtub, but the water was hot and deep and his face remained beneath the surface. My algebraic challenge probably didn't reach his ears, six inches under water fragranced with Radox Floral. The red of his halo paled to rose, tingeing the foam, and then extinguished. Bubbles rose to the surface but Ray the plank didn't float.

It was Dad who pulled me out of the tub. Mum had just stood there screaming until he arrived. My lasting memory, just before my father hurled me across the bathroom and into the tiled wall, was that Ray's superior penis had grown embarrassingly large in his death throes.

I imagine Dad or Mum tried to resuscitate Ray but, if they did, I missed it as the impact against the wall knocked me out cold for a good while. It would have been too late anyway. I had sat on my brother's chest for a good fifteen minutes, fully clothed, wondering what would happen next.

What happened next was my parents lost both their sons. One was drowned; murdered. The other was committed to Fairfield Mental Hospital. I had been exhibiting signs of depression, alternating with bouts of manic behaviour, for some time. I guessed they were referring to me turning over the tables in the classroom when I failed, for the umpteenth time, to get one hundred per cent in the maths test. Little Johnny Maloney always scored one hundred per cent and I could only ever reach ninety-eight. In the unlikely event I ever see Maloney in a bath I won't get my clothes wet. I'll just throw in a live electrical appliance.

I feel no remorse. The act saved me from a life of inferiority and bullying, saved the world from a father's son. And no, God didn't tell me to do it. The deed made perfect sense at the time, and still does. Ray is a much nicer person as a perpetual eleven-year-old than the boorish, philandering sports hero he was destined to become. I preserved his innocence, saved him before our father's purpose could establish itself. Drowning is probably the least painful way I could have done it.

Sorry if I'm sounding like some kind of crazed maniac. This is not a tale of serial murder or any kind of mad mathematician on the rampage. No, this is a story of successful rehabilitation in the community.

The interim

However, my English teacher always complained to me, is not a good way to start a paragraph, let alone a chapter. *But* that was rather a long time ago and such petty rules have since faded in the light of much larger ones. The *Authorities* were the people who disassembled my grammar and *italicised* key parts of my life, through their application of prescription drugs to alleviate the symptoms of my supposed *mental illness*.

These days I rattle like a shaken piggy bank. That's due to myriad pills that transfer weekly from little bottles and blister packs to a plastic morning-noon-evening-night dispenser and then into my stomach.

However, during those earlier days of medication I resembled more a leaking water bomb than a rattling box. Hypodermics oozed their contents into the sloshing bag of bones that had sat on a brother.

The story of my ten years in institutional care: I became fat, my parents died, a Mary shagged me and I was released into the community.

I became fat

Ho, ho. Ray would have pissed himself laughing. It must have been the *Authorities'* drugs. Full self-awareness returned some months after sitting on Ray and I found myself trapped in a fat suit. I belonged in one of those ridiculous films where an alleged comedian portrays an obese professor or a large lady.

'You were always so skinny,' said Mum on her first visit after my return to the world of self-consciousness. It had been three months or so since the deed. 'What are they feeding you in here?'

'They shouldn't feed him at all-uh,' Dad snarled. He had a strange way of ending his sentences-uh.

Dad mourned the demise of capital punishment. The Bedford court had declined his offering me as a sacrifice, pointing out it was nearly half a century since the last hanging. I was surprised Dad hadn't brought a stick with which to poke me from a safe distance.

'And your little face, it's disappeared in there.' She grabbed my jowls with both hands as if I was a chubby baby.

'He still has that dirty hippy hair though-uh,' Dad added, running a hand over his own peach like balding head.

Hair was, indeed, my saving grace. The lank locks I had cultivated before captivity, with the intention of attracting girls and annoying my brother, had somehow escaped the *Authorities'* attention. This hair was subsequently to prove an effective lure for *Marys*.

During the first year of my incarceration I did nothing. That was partially responsible for the obesity. I remained just mobile enough to avoid bed sores. Showering or toilet was the only activity I would willingly indulge in. Even the spoken word I kept to a minimum, begrudging the small energy demanded by speech.

It became a matter of perverse pride to inspect my growing size in the shower. Being small framed, I couldn't carry a lot of weight without the flesh soon forming bulges and rolls. Where skin touched skin, I washed with care. This was not going to be a permanent physical state and I didn't want to emerge from my fat suit some years hence with an incurable skin condition.

My parents died

During his few visits to the nuthouse, as he called it, Dad didn't ever talk to me about Ray, or anything much really. Mum did most of the talking.

'Are they treating you well, dear?'

If treating me well involved drugging me up to the eyeballs, delivering ever increasing amounts of stodge at mealtimes and occasional dodgy blanket baths from a meaty male nurse named *Mary*, then yes, they were treating me well.

'Of course they are, dear, of course they are. Feeding you, that's for sure.'

Mum asked and answered. I looked at Dad and he turned away, half in annoyance with Mum and the other half in revulsion at the killer of his chosen son.

I don't know why Dad visited me. He was there maybe one time in ten compared to Mum and she arrived every week. That means I saw him precisely five times before he died. I do know why he didn't visit nine times out of ten. The same rural Bedfordshire fun park had been his lodgings during an early unsuccessful career as the devil's emissary-uh.

I can imagine Mum and Dad sitting quietly in the front room at home with mugs of tea.

'Barry, you have to ask him. Why bother to visit if you're just going to sit there and snarl?'

'I'll know when the time is right-uh.'

Well, Dad didn't know when the time was right. Mum did. The lid of her pot of impatience was rattling. So she posed the fateful question, the one that had been lurking for a year in Dad's mouth, like a conger eel in its underwater cave.

'Tell us, love, why did you do it? Why did you hurt Ray?'

I didn't *hurt* Ray, I fucking killed the little bastard. She would have to do better than that if I was to break my silence.

'How could you do that to your brother? Kill him, I mean?'

Was Mum seeking a technical explanation for the method of murder? Kneel on the underwater victim's chest until convulsions cease and such details? No, her pleading expression said it was a bigger question. So I told her.

'He had to die, Mum.'

They both recoiled as though I had cracked a whip.

'Had to die?' She repeated in a small, high voice. Then softly, 'Why?'

'Surely you saw it, what he was becoming?'

'Saw it? What he was becoming?'

Mum the parrot.

'I can't believe you were oblivious to it. The bullying, the boasting, the strutting.'

She pulled a face that would have told a waiter the food was unfit for human consumption. Dad's eyes fixed me like a mongoose facing a python.

'You know what *he* is. Ray was turning into *him*!' I raised one fat hand, with some effort, and pointed my forefinger at Dad. He looked over his shoulder at *Mary* and I laughed.

'Him?' Mum was incredulous. 'You killed Ray because he was turning into a male nurse?'

'No, you idiot!' I had never said that to my mother before. 'He was turning into his chosen son.'

'Don't call your mother an idiot-uh!' were the last words Dad addressed to me. He was escorted from the premises by security. My jaw wasn't broken, probably the fat face had protected it, but my nose was. Like I said, Ray had been in the process of turning into Dad.

Mum, Dad and I all knew what that meant.

So, they went home, thought it over and then killed themselves. Well, Dad did all the shooting. I was surprised. I didn't realise he had a shotgun or even knew how to use one. Their suicide pact made a big splash in the media, as these things do. The quality papers used the word fratricide to explain what had driven a respectable middle aged couple to such a bloody end.

It was their decision. Dad's life purpose had been proven void. And his works had been successfully frustrated by yours truly. But I was not totally unaffected by the trauma. I regained my sense of smell.

Things not Done

Bless me father, for I abandoned your concept of sin half a lifetime ago. Here is my confession.

I sin when I break my own code. Each breach demands remorse and penance. Each sin is not of something done but of things not done. Words unsaid, actions left uncommitted.

Society would judge me if I struck down, took life, abandoned monogamy. So I don't. Let my characters commit the sins of society and pay the price. My sin is lack of courage, but I excuse this and call it conscience.

Martha Woodcock

I was born in Kilkenny and have been writing for over twenty years. I wrote a regular column in the Kilkenny Standard in the 1990s and spent some time working in the Times Literary Supplement in London. I have had poems and short stories published in the Irish Times, the Kilkenny Broadsheet and the Bray Arts Journal. Last year I performed at Listowel Writers' Week. I have travelled extensively and have lived in New Orleans and New York. I have drawn much inspiration from a six week voluntary stint in Kenya, fundraising and working with people who possess nothing, but remain full of hope. I am privileged to teach in St. Patrick's De la Salle, Kilkenny. In difficult times I work at remaining optimistic about the goodness and generosity of people.

22

As Good as Gold

by Martha Woodcock

My granny was called Muddy for short. And the name stuck. Granddad, in contrast was a giant of a man, with moustache, large brown bowler hat almost faded to green, a thorny walking stick and a pipe at the side of his mouth during his waking hours. We called him Da. Muddy and Da lived in 'The Bungalow,' and to this day I don't know why we called it that. Modern and slate roofed was a million miles away from what this house was.

Magic happened in the Bungalow. My grandparents loved company, so visits were very special. It was old world and I remember when my four cousins came from Dublin. They always got to stay. My sister and I were really jealous. But in the summer, we were allowed sleep there for a night when they were down. We stayed at other times when there wasn't such a crowd around but we loved the night with the cousins. There was one big double bed in the spare room between us all; three would take up one end and three the other, just the odd toe meeting in the middle. A bit of heckling with feet would start when we got into bed first. We soon settled into telling stories. Of their school in Dublin, of the songs they learned. We hadn't heard of half of them. They laughed when we told them of our two teacher school in the village.

Life sounded exciting in Dublin. I was dying to visit. But we had to wait for an invitation. That was what my mother said any time I pleaded with her.

'But I want to go and see their house Mam.'

My mother calmed me, telling me that once we got the invite we would take the train and go for as long as I wanted. I didn't believe her. Sometimes she made wild promises to shut me up and I reckoned this was one of them.

When we settled in the bed that night, Maura, the eldest of the four, but a year younger than me, interrupted our counting of who had how many dolls.

'I wonder if there's any ghost here?'

Silence fell in the dim light that came through the pane of glass at the top of the door from the light in the hall outside.

'What do you mean?' I questioned bravely.

'Dad told me that the Bungalow was much cheaper than they thought it would be. Nobody would buy it – meant to be a woman wandering around at night.'

I laughed out loud.

'Come off it, nobody's ever seen a ghost here.'

'How do you know – did you ever ask?'

I hadn't ever asked anybody. Come on, I was eleven years old. This was my grandparents' house. I was getting to stay here as the biggest treat in the world and my jackeen cousin was destroying it for me. Some of the younger cousins weren't so brave. Padraig started crying and said he wanted the light on. Maura switched on the tiny lamp that was sitting on a little dark wooden locker beside the bed. She told him she was only joking. The laughter died down after that and we decided to leave the light on all night for Padraig. It wasn't really just for him. Somehow, all six of us managed to fall asleep, and woke the next morning to bright August sunshine.

We scrambled from the bed, took off our pyjamas and put on the fresh clothes that my mother had put on the musty shelf for Jane and me. My cousins organised themselves, Maura sorting the younger ones in the corner of the room to give the boys their privacy. We had just slept in the same bed, but changing clothes was a more delicate matter. When we went down the small hall, Muddy was standing at the fire and the kettle was whistling. We sat in to a feast of brown bread that she had made the night before, dollops of homemade raspberry jam and big mugs of hot milky tea. This was great. This was why we loved coming. Da came into the flagstone kitchen, took one look at all of us around the table, stretched his arms up over his head and walked out the back door.

'He's gone to check the hens, he won't be long,' Muddy announced.

After breakfast, we cleared away the dishes but she refused help with the washing up. She had her own way of doing things and told us to go and get a bit of fresh air.

Her hair, as always, in a neat bun, tied up with long, uncomfortable looking steel pins. Outside, I was looking forward to showing the others everything at the back of the house.

There was a sense of the exotic about the Bungalow and there was a tank a few yards from the back door. Sometimes we sat on the edge of it and splashed around a bit. When nobody was looking. It was at the entrance to the big bamboo wood that was all overgrown. Just as I was leading the way to it, Da came back holding four or five eggs comfortably in each hand.

'Be careful with that water, it's much deeper than it looks.'

We had been well warned. Every time we came to the Bungalow, Da said the same thing.

'Remember what I told you before. Don't go near it.'

We promised we wouldn't but went to take a look all the same.

'What's the big deal about it? Nothing special if you ask me.' Hannah moaned.

I felt embarrassed as I had checked out all sorts around the house and the garden to show them when they'd come and here I was trying to make a tank of rainwater seem as significant as the Niagara Falls we'd heard about in school.

'I didn't say it was special, just nice to see the frogspawn on it in the spring and sometimes you'd see frogs around it.'

'Yeah, yeah. Come on,' Maura interrupted.

She made most of the decisions when she was down, where we would go and when. That annoyed me. Jane liked playing with Padraig and Barry and didn't really notice how bossy Maura was.

We made our way over to the path and off we went. Within a few yards of entering the garden, there were bamboos criss crossing overhead and, although the sun was shining, the light was already dim.

When we got back to the house, Da had been looking for us.

'Any mushrooms down there today?'

I had forgotten to get them and I knew how much he loved them for his tea, grilled with a knob of butter melting away in the middle and a pinch of salt on the top.

'You can't beat a good mushroom, I always say.'

Da smiled. We loved him. And loved when he'd give us money and we'd head down the road to the local pub that served as a shop as well.

'Pick up the batch bread for later and keep the change, get something for everyone. One after the other now. Be careful on that road.'

We didn't have to be told twice. And like ducks, the six of us headed off down the road, in single file to avoid the odd car and into Nell Brennan's pub half a mile away. Though Muddy was a great baker and cook, she only liked making brown bread.

'I don't know what Hickey's put in the bread but I can't make it the same,' she often muttered.

Nell was a wiry woman. Skinny and bony looking and we thought she must be a hundred. Later I learned she was only about sixty. But everybody seemed ancient when we were young.

Five pence each, doled out to everyone once I had paid for the bread. And then it started. What to pick. Nell was an impatient woman and had jobs to do. She'd have left us there until we had all decided what we wanted except she didn't trust children. Pity really, because she made more money from sweets than anything else. She didn't have much in the way of supplies, just emergency stuff like bread and tea. Even then, most people went to town.

'I don't know why they bother with town at all, cycling six miles in and six back when you get everything you want here,' she complained to Da one day when we were with him.

That was when she sold bacon and cooked corned beef, cheese and a few buns that she'd make herself. No point anymore since nobody bought them. But none of this helped us. Six children, shifting from foot to foot, deciding between two bags of Perri crisps that were two and a half pence each or summer drinks, a flavoured powder that you added water to in order to change it into a fizzy concoction that was magical. Lemon was my favourite.

They were a penny. I finally settled on one of each and three halfpenny toffee sweets. Eventually everyone got what they wanted and happily we left, back to the Bungalow. Nell Brennan told Muddy that she often closed the shop for an hour after a gang of children had been.

'I'm not able for them. They're so slow to make up their minds. Sometimes I just take their change and give them their money's worth to get rid of them. They don't like it. But I don't have the day to be serving them.'

She had to divide her day between the shop, the pub and generally minding the house. Keeping an eye out for anyone who might be trying to rob her. She liked to have a tight rein on the place and she didn't like it when strangers stopped in out of the blue. Even the cousins had to be cross examined before she relaxed a bit with them.

There was a lot of laughing on the way home and we talked about what we'd got. We walked in twos till we got to the Bungalow. Da wouldn't be happy but he'd never know.

'Nell is an oul cow,' Maura piped up.

'She's not that bad. Just old.' I said.

'I'll bring in the bread; wait for me at the tank.'

I lifted the latch on the back door and placed the bread on the bare wooden kitchen table. Everything had been tidied away. Muddy smiled.

'I hope ye weren't driving Nell mad down there.'

'We were as good as gold Muddy. As good as gold.'

Unfilled Spaces

Dark black tight cut hair. She used stark words.

Matter of fact. Lots of gaps between. Ryan Tubridy didn't try to fill the spaces. Sparse words of how she was primed, how she was abused, spilled into the silences. The man's name stated. Over and over.

Sadness laced the silence. She stayed strong: resolute in the telling of her story. A seven year sentence ended after five months. The audience filled the silence with deep sighs. Unanimously.

Silence needs space. Just to be. To let the story be told.

Without interruption.

Directive

La y sin where it belongs:
at the feet of the sinner.
Remove it from your heart.
Do not waste another second
of your precious life.
Move swiftly.

Francis Mc Manus 2011
Miner: Austin Duffey - Orca